Wine From The Wilds

WINE FROM THE WILDS

Using Wild Trees, Herbs, and Flowers in Home Winemaking

Steven A. Krause

Illustrations by Robert W. Freckmann

Stackpole Books

WINE FROM THE WILDS

Copyright © 1982 by Steven A. Krause

Published by
STACKPOLE BOOKS
Cameron and Kelker Streets
P.O. Box 1831
Harrisburg, Pa. 17105

Published simultaneously in Scarborough, Ontario, Canada
by Thomas Nelson & Sons, Ltd.

Printed in the U.S.A.

Library of Congress Cataloging in Publication Data

Krause, Steven A.
  Wine from the wilds.

  Bibliography: p.
  Includes index.
  1. Wine and winemaking—Amateurs' manuals.
  2. Plants, Useful. I. Title.
TP548.2.K73   1982   641.8'72   81-16685
  ISBN 0-8117-2129-9   AACR2

To Bob and Sally Freckmann,
whose passion for wild plants rubbed off

Contents

Wine drunk with moderation is the joy of the soul and heart.
Ecclesiasticus 31:36

Preface

Most home winemakers buy the sugar, yeast, oranges, and the main ingredient for their wine in a supermarket. They may buy a concentrate specifically made for winemaking or a concentrated fruit juice meant for drinking. More likely, they will buy several pounds of fresh grapes, apples, or cranberries to start their wine.

Since making wine is as much fun as drinking it, I feel these winemakers are missing a lot by not collecting the ingredients fresh from the field, from vines, trees, or shrubs. From gathering tree sap in the chilly weather of March or April, to picking mint in the heat of July, to collecting rosehips in late fall, collecting expeditions can be well worth the effort.

Each bottle of wild wine will have memories poured into it. When you sample your blueberry wine in February, you will recall bluffing that bear away from the blueberry patch, even though you left most of the berries for him. Or, as you taste your blackberry wine, you may still wish you hadn't worn shorts that day, no matter how warm it was.

Another reason to gather your own wild ingredients is that more types of wine can be produced. Unlike cultivated plants, which come in purebred varieties, wild plants are quite variable. This is obvious to anyone who has seen a patch of wild apple trees. Even though they are all the same species, every tree has different characteristics. Wine made with apples from one tree will be different than wine made with apples from another. Mixing apples from many trees will increase the variety of flavors.

In addition, some groups have many species, and each species will be slightly different in flavor from every other. Furthermore, there are often hybrids and intergrades that will also be slightly different.

Location can make a difference. Fruits growing in sunny locations produce tastes different from those grown in shady ones. Plants growing in swamps would be different from those found on dry land. Soil and climate also make a difference. So if you make an unusually good batch of wine, remember where you gathered the ingredients. It may be a prize patch, so don't tell any fellow winemakers, or they might clean it out before you get there next year.

Though some winemakers (and wine drinkers) insist that a fermented beverage made from something other than grapes is not wine, other winemakers (and wine drinkers) prefer the numerous other kinds of wine that can be made. Cranberry wine is highly esteemed by some, and violet wine was very popular with the ancient Romans. And according to one authority, the best wine to take ice fishing is blackberry. By experimenting, you may find wines you prefer to grape wine, too. If not, they will at least be great conversation wines.

And how abundant are these wild ingredients? It depends on the part of the country you are in, whether it is a large city, a farm area, or a wild area with waste places. My parents have a cottage in a sterile, sandy, oak wood in northern Wisconsin. Within a quarter of a mile are harvestable patches of blackberries, dewberries, blueberries, cherries (two types), raspberries, strawberries, and juneberries. On river islands in our city are currants, elderberries, and mint. The lawns are full of dandelions, violets, and chickweed. I have stumbled onto other edible and fermentable plant species while hiking, bicycling, fishing and hunting nearby. Some of you will not be as lucky, others may be luckier.

This book is written for home winemakers who have access to some wild ingredients and who are inventive enough to try them. It is intended as a sort of field botany book for experienced and beginner winemakers. But it should not be the sole wine book in your library. Neither should it be the sole botany book in your library. Until you learn to recognize a species of plant, initial identification can be tricky. Since some plants are poisonous, it would be possible to make wine out of misidentified poisonous plants.

As an example, I once spied a bed of low-growing herbs in the mud next to a cold-water stream. They seemed to fit the description Euell Gibbons gave in one of his books for watercress. I put two leaves in my mouth, and found they had a bitter taste, not a pungent one, so I spit them out. Later I found out it was pennywort (*Hydrocotyle*), a toxic herb. If I had eaten a quantity, it would have made me sick.

So get one or two books on plant identification. The best one for the northeastern United States is *A Field Guide to Wildflowers*. Also, *A Field Guide to Trees and Shrubs* will cover the woody plants. There are also books for other areas of the country and some books to help in identifying plants of individual states.

The plants covered in this book will be found primarily in the northeastern United States. Many of them have related species in other parts of the country. My ultimate authority is the *Manual of Vascular Plants* by Gleason and Cronquist.

Recipes can be found in home winemaking books for all of the plant groups described here. For some of the groups, my father or a friend have made their own homemade wine, so I present their recipes.

Just as there is a great diversity of wild plant species that wine can be made from, so can the recipes be varied to increase further the variety in your wine cellar. The experimentation can go on for your lifetime. So grab your plastic bag or pail, and let us head for the hills.

I would like to thank several people who were instrumental in producing this book: Bill Evenson, who suggested the book; Albert Krause, my father, who made numerous wines before and after the idea; Jean Krause, my mother, who typed the book; Dave and Carolyn Stachovak, who helped with the photographs; and Bob Freckmann, who made the drawings.

Chapter One

Basic Winemaking

A BRIEF HISTORY

Winemaking, or viticulture, has come a long way since its origins in the mountains of Armenia. The original wine grape, *Vitis vinifera*, still grows there. Most cultivated species of grapes are descended from this.

According to the book of Genesis, Noah landed the ark on Mount Ararat, also in the mountains of Armenia. When the waters receded, he planted a vineyard. He made wine from the grapes which grew there and proceeded to get drunk from it. Could Noah have thought highly enough of wine to carry grape seeds aboard the ark? And are these the ancestors of most of the commercial wine grapes alive today?

Winemaking is known to have spread from Armenia to Mesopotamia about 5,000 years ago. The wine grape was the ingredient again for one good reason. Grapes naturally have the right combination of juices, sugars, and pectins; and their skins have wild yeasts on them. The climate was warm in that area, so one had only to mash ripe grapes in a vessel, wait a few weeks, strain off the pulp, and the wine was ready.

Winemaking later spread to Egypt, where the fertile soil and bright sunshine in the Nile Valley produced a bounty of wine grapes. The first wine connoisseurs were in Egypt, classifying various qualities and types of wine. Later winemaking spread to Greece and Italy, and then to the rest of Europe.

In Europe other kinds of wine were developed over the centuries. Germany, Spain, and France all have long traditions of making non-grape fruit wines. For centuries the English have gathered many fruits and flowers for making wines. (Indeed, many home wine-making books today have English authors.) The English colonists brought their fondness for these wines to America. Their recipes have been handed down from one generation to the next, each one adding to or changing the variety of recipes.

HOW TO MAKE WINE

Winemaking at home is very simple and not very time consuming. The necessary supplies can be acquired very cheaply. The space needed is minimal; a corner of the basement can become your wine cellar.

Let us go through a generalized procedure for making wine, discussing equipment and events on the way. This simplified procedure cannot be used with all types of ingredients, but it will serve as an introduction to winemaking.

First, you will need a five or ten gallon capacity pail. It should be plastic or earthenware, but definitely not metal. Metal could be hazardous. Aluminum or copper, by being dissolved or oxidized into the brew, could hamper fermentation. Lead glaze could also mix into the brew, making the wine unhealthy to drink.

A wood or plastic stirring stick is also needed.

Put the required amount of ingredients in the bottom of the pail. Boil water (usually a gallon), and pour it over the ingredients. Add the stated amount of white sugar and stir to dissolve it. At this point, some recipes may call for the addition of raisins, oranges, or lemons.

The best container for closed fermentation of wine is a one-gallon glass jug. This will enable you to check color, clarity, and rate of fermentation easily. Plastic or clay jugs can also be used, but metal and metallic-glazed jugs should be avoided.

Also in some cases it may be necessary to add a *campden tablet* at this time. This will sterilize the potion and prevent the growth of mold and other undesirable microbes.

Allow the mixture to cool for twenty-four hours before adding the yeast. Adding yeast to the mixture while it is still hot would probably kill the yeast. Waiting also allows the effect of the campden tablet to wear off. When the mixture, called *must*, is at room temperature, add the wine yeast. Bakers' yeast can be used, but is not recommended. Wine yeast, available in hobby shops, has been specially bred for winemaking and has a much better chance of producing good results.

Once the yeast has been added, keep the must in a fairly warm place and cover it with cheesecloth to keep out the dust and dirt. Fermentation will begin and should be allowed to continue for the time specified in the recipe (often 7 to 10 days). Stir the must once a day.

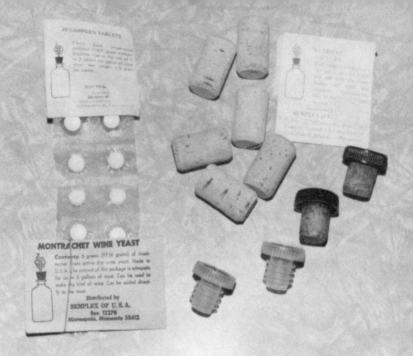

Wine yeasts, yeast nutrients, campden tablets, and corks are some of the wine-making supplies commonly sold in hobby shops. Citric acid, used as a substitute for lemon and orange juice; clearing agents, such as pectinase; and mechanical aids, such as siphon hoses, corkers, cork screws, and fermentation locks, are also available.

The fermentation lock or water-seal keeps oxygen out of the must, allowing maximum alcohol production, and at the same time allows the rapidly forming carbon dioxide to escape.

To rack wine, siphon it to another jug, being careful to leave the bottom sediments in the fermentation jug.

When the wine in the aging vessel has cleared and aged enough, siphon it into bottles.

When the wine has sufficiently cleared in the fermentation jug, transfer it into bottles for aging. When using a clay jug, first siphon out a little to check clarity. Then mark the distance to the bottom on the hose to avoid siphoning up bottom sediments.

There are several types of corkers on the market to assist in getting the cork into
the bottle. However, it still requires effort. Soak, and preferably boil, the cork to
help it slide in and to help insure a proper fit. Properly corked bottles should have
the cork shoved most or all of the way in, leaving it just a bit above or flush with
the mouth of the bottle. There should be an inch or two of air in the neck of the
bottle between the bottom of the cork and the surface of the wine.

Bottles of wine stored for a long time should be laid on their sides, so that the wine wets the bottom of the cork. If a cork dries out, it could shrink, break the seal, and possibly lead to contamination of the wine.

Fermentation is a form of food utilization without oxygen. Most plants and animals require oxygen to derive energy from sugar, giving off carbon dioxide and water. Some yeasts and bacteria do not require oxygen for their energy requirements. Yeast, a microscopic plant, can survive for long periods without oxygen. They break down sugar into a small amount of carbon dioxide and a lot of alcohol.

This process keeps the microscopic yeast cells alive but is not usually sufficient to increase their numbers. Oxygen is required for that, though the presence of oxygen decreases fermentation.

The purpose of keeping the must in an open pail is not only to extract the juices and flavors from the main ingredient, but to allow the living yeast cells to reproduce in large numbers. Fermentation is limited in this stage, but it has begun.

To start the wine fermenting on a large scale, remove it from the presence of oxygen. Strain the liquid from the residue into a glass jug, filling the jug nearly to the top. Place a *fermentation lock* or *water seal* in the mouth of the jug. This winemaker's gadget allows carbon dioxide to escape from the wine freely while preventing oxygen from entering.

Place the fermentation jug in a warm place so the mixture can ferment on a grand scale. Bubbles will rise out of the mixture for six weeks or longer. In some cases, if the bubbling slows down, small amounts of sugar can be added to increase the fermentation, but this will also increase the alcohol content. When the bubbles have ceased completely, the sugar is all gone or the yeast have died.

Then carefully rack the wine into an *aging vessel*. Racking is the careful siphoning of the fermented wine into another glass jug, using a plastic hose. Let the wine sit until it clears. When it does, carefully siphon the clear wine into wine bottles, cork them and label them as to type and date of manufacture.

Tasting the wine at this time will determine if it is ready to drink. Most wines require six months to two years of aging in the wine cellar. Be sure to make enough to last longer than two years. Most wines continue to improve in quality for many years while aging. You may wish to let a few bottles of a particularly good vintage age a long time.

There are many variations on the general recipe given here. These are the results of experimentation. Some main ingredients require that some things be done differently. In other cases, someone succeeded in fitting a recipe to the equipment or ingredients at hand. In still other cases, someone decided to add oranges or raisins. While there are many failures in winemaking experiments, there are also many successes, which have led to the present state of the art.

When shall I awake, and find wine again?
Proverbs 23:35

Chapter Two

Identifying Wild Plants

In order to properly collect the main ingredient in a wild wine, you must be able to correctly identify the plant, tree, or shrub in question. Some may be readily recognizable, such as the strawberry or dandelion. Others may not be recognizable even to trained botanists. These would include some species of dewberries and many hawthorns, which are quite difficult to differentiate.

Most kinds of wild plants can be identified readily with practice, however. If you already know some kinds, you are well ahead of the game. You may have others pointed out by someone knowledgeable in wild plants. Study these very carefully, so you recognize them again. Many a farm grandma is adept at recognizing wild plants by their local common names. With a little help from such a person, many hours of identifying by textbook can be saved.

To identify a plant using a textbook, it is important to collect a specimen of the plant. If it is an herbaceous plant, collect the whole plant when it is in flower. If it is a tree, shrub, or woody vine, a branch with leaves, flowers, or fruits will suffice.

The flower is usually the most important part for identification of species. Fruits do not always distinguish closely related species, and leaves of different kinds of plants can look much alike. But the flower readily shows the difference. However, in most trees and shrubs, the fruits and leaves and bark will be enough to identify the species.

Most plant identification books use what is called a dichotomous key to the species. This key divides the subject into sections and subsections and more subsections until the species is reached. As an example, assume you have a plant specimen in hand:

1. Plant green, soft, and herbaceous throughout . . . . Herbs
1. Plant hard and woody . . . . see #2
   2. Plant climbing or trailing . . . . Vine
   2. Plant not climbing or trailing, erect . . . . see #3
      3. Plant very tall, thick stem . . . . Tree
      3. Plant only a few feet tall, bushy . . . . Shrub

This key might make a botanist shriek, but it illustrates the principle used in all plant keys: divide everything into two groups on the basis of one characteristic. Either the plant is woody or it is not. That places it in one group or the other. If it is woody, continue through the key to determine just what kind of woody plant it is. Finally you will reach an ultimate end which should give a description that fits the plant in hand. If the detailed description does not match the specimen, you made a wrong choice somewhere up the key and you must start over.

Sometimes keying a plant specimen can take a long time. However, once it is identified correctly after all that effort, you will never forget that particular species. Every characteristic is memorized.

Plant identification books written for botanists contain keys that are often much too difficult for the amateur. Avoid these books. Find books written specifically for amateurs. Their keys are usually in relatively simple English, and they contain glossaries to explain the botanist-ese which inevitably appears.

For instance, *A Field Guide to Wildflowers* contains a very simple key. The wildflowers are arranged in sections based on flower color. For each color, there are sub-groupings based on easily determined characteristics, such as flower shape. Opposite each page of description there are line drawings pointing out the key characteristics of each plant. If the plant is in there, anyone can find it easily.

Another source of easy plant keys is reference manuals that cover only limited areas, such as *The Flora of Michigan* and *Spring Flora of Wisconsin*. These books only list species known to occur in the area being covered. The process of keying is much easier lessening the chance of a mistake. These books often have drawings and glossaries as well.

Plants are grouped into large groups called *families*. Each *species* in a family has major structures in common. For example, the mint family is a large family, including spearmint, peppermint, and catnip. Each species has square stems, opposite leaves, and in most cases, its own type of minty fragrance. The flowers are also very similar.

Learning the primary characteristics of a plant family can save a lot of identifying. If you see a plant with square stems and opposite leaves, crinkle up a leaf, smell it and say, "This is a mint!" Then open your book to find the next subgrouping, the *genus*. The mint may be of the genus *Mentha*, which is comprised of a number of species. Key it further and you might find your species to be *Mentha arvensis*, true mint; *Mentha spicata*, spearmint; or *Mentha piperata*, peppermint.

Sometimes species are further subdivided into *varieties*. These are often geographical. It may be only a difference in amount of hair on the stems; sometimes the differences are more radical. However, learning what plant species you have found should be as far as the average winemaker need go.

If you cannot identify a plant, press and dry the specimen between newspapers and cardboards. When it is flat and dry, take it or mail it to a college or museum that has a plant collection, or herbarium. The staff will try to identify it for you.

A visit to a local herbarium can also provide clues as to whether certain winemaking plants grow in your area. Each pressed plant has data regarding the place of collection. If the herbarium does not have a record of a particular species coming from your area, you may have to get it elsewhere.

The herbarium also provides clues to local blooming dates, fruiting dates, and soil and habitat for the species. A winemaker can acquire much information from a regional public plant collection.

The information thus acquired can tell you approximately when and where to look. But you still must go into the field, collecting bag in hand, seeking the ingredient for your wine. Develop a sharp eye to spot that gooseberry bush in the woods, that apple tree in a field, or that mint patch in a marsh. When nothing escapes you in the field and you can identify the plants you find to your satisfaction, then you are on the way to becoming expert and safe at making wine from the wilds.

A new friend is as new wine: it shall grow old
and thou shalt drink it with pleasure.
Ecclesiasticus 9:14

Chapter Three

Fruit Wines

Wine was first made from grapes because they had all the necessary ingredients. Then, with experimentation, people found that fine wines could be made from many other kinds of fruit. The bilberry of Europe is popular as a wine. A sparkling apple wine is made in Spain. Wine recipes can be found for damsons, sloes, and greengages (three European types of plums). There are wine recipes for apricots, dates, figs, lemons, limes, oranges, peaches, pears, and pineapples.

Different types of fruits have different amounts of the necessary winemaking components, so the recipes have to be varied to adjust.

One substance that many fruits are high in is *pectin*, the substance found between the cell walls of fruits and other soft plant parts that holds the cell walls together and yields a gel that is the basis of jams and jellies. This is generally undesirable in wine, as the pectin tends to act to keep all the molecules in suspension, called a *colloidal solution*. The pectin prevents the minute particles from settling out so the wine remains a colloidal solution and does not clear. However, depectinizing enzymes can be purchased which break down the pectin and prevent the problem. While most fruits contain some pectin, those particularly high in pectin include plums, crabapples, gooseberries, and currants. So, recipes may call for addition of the depectinizing enzyme, pectinase.

Another substance that various fruits have in different quantities is tannin or tannic acid. This is present in tree leaves and bark (especially oak) and also in the skins of most fruits. Wines with a small amount or no tannin, such as flower wines, sometimes call for it to be added, to add zest or bite to the taste. In the case of fruit wines, the bite can be excessive, a prime reason for aging the wine before drinking. The tannin eventually break down to a manageable level.

A third factor to consider is acidity. Many fruits like lemons and tomatoes are extremely acid. In order to make them more drinkable as wine, a lot of sugar must be added. This will make them sweet wines and appropriate for dinner or dessert.

In most cases, harvest fruits when they are ripe. Go through them later at home to remove semi-ripe, overripe, decayed, dehydrated, or bird-eaten fruits. Also all stems, leaves, caterpillars, and spiders should be removed. It is difficult and time consuming to do this while picking the fruit.

Wash the fruit in cold water and start the winemaking process as soon as possible. After fruit is picked, the sugars, proteins, and enzymes start to break down, slowly at first. To get the full benefit of the fruit into the finished wine, start the winemaking immediately after picking.

Do not expect a fruit wine to taste like the fresh juice of the fruit. All sorts of things go on in the process of turning juice into wine. The finished product may not be at all recognizable as coming from that fruit. If you want it to taste like fruit juice, drink it while it is still fruit juice.

A few fruits do let their flavors get through. Raspberries and strawberries, for examples, make excellent wines, which can be recognized as coming from the fruit.

If you are a beginning winemaker and would rather not try wild fruit as your first attempt at winemaking, try one of the fruits sold in a supermarket. The first attempt at winemaking is crucial to building confidence. If it works, future success is assured. After that, try a wild fruit.

WILD GRAPES

The original ancestor of the present grape vineyards was a wild species, *Vitis vinifera*, that was carried by man from Armenia to Egypt to Europe. It is far from being the only grape species in existence. Many more wild kinds are found throughout the United States.

Grapevines were noted by Leif Erikson and other travelers from Scandinavia a thousand years ago. At that time, the Norse colony on the west coast of Greenland was thriving. Recent evidence suggests they also had camps in Newfoundland and Quebec. Sailing down the New England coast, they were amazed to find the coasts filled with wild grapes. Since they probably had never seen them before (outside of cultivated vineyards) but knew what they were used for, the wild grapes were remembered and included in the Norse sagas. No more expeditions to the new Vineland were made, and the Greenland colony inexplicably vanished. Only the tales remained of a mysterious western land where grapes grew wild.

Hundreds of years later, the English colonists began to show up in America. They also noticed the wild grapes, and attempted to make wine from them. Apparently they did not succeed, for they were soon importing grapevines from Europe. (Perhaps they wanted to use what they were sure of in the harsh new land.) However, the European grapes were coaxed without success for 200 years.

The reason for the failure was a small parasitic louse that infected the roots of many American species. The American species had resistance to the louse from long association. The imported grapevines had no resistance and were readily infected, since the cultivated grapes usually were planted near the wild ones.

The only place imported grapes succeeded was in California, where there were no lice. They eventually found their way there, however, and even made their way to Europe, where they ravaged the vineyards in the nineteenth century.

Eventually the rootstocks of the resistant American species were grafted to the vines of European varieties. This saved the European and Californian vineyards, and allowed European grapes to be grown

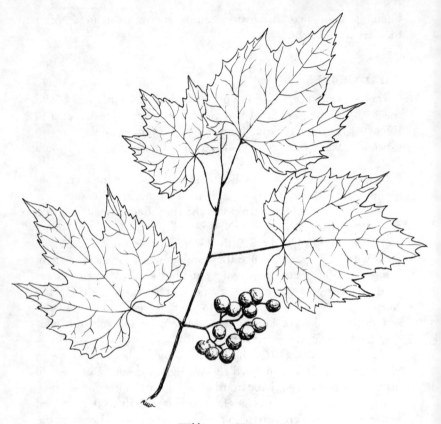

Wild grape; *Vitis*

in this country. Most vineyard wines are still made from European
varieties, with few varieties developed from wild American species.
Wild grapes probably wouldn't satisfy wine connoisseurs, but they
may satisfy most home winemakers.

All wild grapes, whether sweet or sour, can be used in jelly, pie,
and juice. Many wild grapes can be eaten raw, including the Mus-
cadine grape (*Vitis rotundifolia*), the ancestor of the cultivated Scup-
pernong grape. Even the leaves can be eaten.

Ten species of wild grapes are described from the northeastern

United States alone. They all look somewhat similar, so you may
want to refer to an identification manual to differentiate them. They
are all of the genus *Vitis* and are in the same family as the Virginia
Creeper.

Wild grapes are found along roadsides, in thickets and on riverbanks. The one species common to my area, the Riverbank grape
(*Vitis riparia*), is almost exclusively a stream-bank species. It can
grow a thick vine that is so heavy it bends over the tree it is growing
on. The leaves are sometimes so numerous and thick that they cut
off the sunlight from the tree leaves, killing the tree.

The harvest of wild grapes is unpredictable. Many grapevines
produce few or no grapes because a lot of sunshine is required for
grape production. A shady location or poor weather at a crucial time
stifles production. Still, these vines are numerous and some do fruit.

I located a vine with a rich harvest one September. The fruits
were small and black with a whitish bloom. They were growing in
tight clusters that I cut off the vine with a wire cutter to avoid
damaging the vine. That vine produced not quite so abundantly the
next year and not at all last year.

These grapes produced an excellent full-bodied wine. It may have
just been a vintage year or I may have found a particularly good
wild grape vine. Whatever the case, winemakers wanted to know
where the vine was. They never found out.

Other wild grapes can be used to make good wines. Euell Gibbons
used a recipe similar to the following one to make excellent wines
from mustang grapes (*Vitis candicans*) and fox grapes (*Vitis la-
brusca*). He was not a wine lover, but for these he made an exception.

Seek out the wild grape populations near you. Tangles of woody
vines climbing a tree may be a clue in winter. If the vine is large
and the bark peels off lengthwise, it is probably a grape. Tight little
tendrils are another winter clue.

In summer, look for leaves of variable shape, depending on species, and the peeling bark and tendrils. In August, locate vines with
green fruit. Then be ready when they are ripe a month or so later.
Keeping track of several patches of wild grapes will help insure
against a particular vine or patch failing one year.

After your first wild grape wine has cleared and aged, and you
are tasting it for the first time, think of the history of the American

wild grape. Think of the people who imported European grapes because they had no love for native grapes. And think back a thousand years to the rugged sailors of Leif Erikson, so confounded by the abundance of wild grapes in the new land.

Making Wild Grape Wine

Pick about five pounds of grapes. Remove them from the clusters carefully, for spiders like to hide there. Then rinse them.

Put two cups of grapes in the bottom of a plastic pail. Add one cup of sugar. Keep adding two cups of grapes and one cup of sugar until you run out of grapes. Do *not* mash the grapes.

Cover this with warm water and let it stand for three days at room temperature.

Add the yeast and let it work ten to twelve days to build up the yeast population.

Strain the liquid into a fermentation jug, seal it with a water-seal, and let it work to completion, two or three months. The wine should clear by itself.

Siphon to an aging vessel, and age for six months to one year.

CURRANTS

Currants are a favorite for winemaking in England. There are different cultivated plants grown there and here in the United States that will produce black, red, or white currants. There are some recipes for black currants, others for red currants, and still others for white. Some recipes require equal parts of each.

Currents tend to have a northerly range and so are not found in the far south. There are eight species of currants growing in the northeastern United States. Some of these are rare escapees, where the seeds of a cultivated bush have scattered and grown on their own. Most species are native and found in cool moist woods.

Currants are small bushes, one to (rarely) two meters tall. They have small, somewhat maple-shaped leaves. Their branches frequently arch outward with small flowers and, later, fruits hanging down them. The fruits ripen in July and August and drop off when they get overripe. Birds often prevent this, however.

These characteristics are shared with gooseberries. They are all part of the genus *Ribes*, the currants being smooth, red, or black and the gooseberries, green or purple-brown, and sometimes spiny.

Currants in the United States come in two colors, black and red. The black currant (*Ribes nigrum*) is a garden bush from Europe sometimes found in the wild. The same is true of the garden currant with red fruits (*Ribes sativum*).

Two native species also have red fruit. One, the skunk currant, is a northern species found in swamps and wet places. It is one of the earliest plants to start blooming in spring, with insignificant flowers. The fruits have a disagreeable odor, so it is not a good one for wine. This plant is very low, often sprawling in the water. Its size and the skunk-like odor of the fruits will distinguish this bush from the more desirable currants.

The other native species is the swamp red currant (*Ribes triste*). Found in wet woods and swamps from Canada south across the northern United States, it grows erect and somewhat straggling, usually only one meter tall. The ripe fruits can be gathered in late July or August.

In addition to the red currants, several native black currants can be found. The Hudson Bay black currant is found almost entirely in Canada. The common black currant (*Ribes americanum*) is similar and found farther south.

Another black currant, the swamp black currant (*Ribes lacustre*) can be distinguished from the other black currants, as it is the only one with branches protected by short spines. To make it worse, the short spines are protected by longer, stouter spines. However, the ripe fruits are far enough from the spines to avoid them when picking.

The swamp black currant is found in Canada and the northern tier of the United States. As its name implies, it is found in swamps and river bottomlands.

Beware of the hazards of picking currants in these wet areas. I found out the hard way while searching for swamp black currants along the Wisconsin River. It was a hot day at the end of July when I descended into some wild river bottom swamps. I spent hours searching through tangles of vines, bedstraw, and especially nettles. As currants have a nasty way of ripening only two inches above the nearest nettle plants, I ended up with quite itchy hands. Also, by plunging through swamp underbrush, I awakened clouds of sleeping

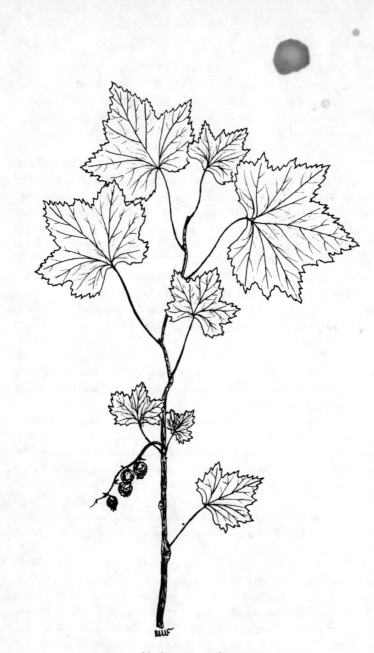

American black current; *Ribes americanum*

mosquitoes. These proceeded to bite my hands around the nettle stab wounds, making me doubly itchy.

Pick only the ripe fruits. When they get too ripe, they drop off anyway. Discard any fruits that the birds have pecked open.

Currants are used for other things in addition to wine. Cultivated currants are used for pies and jellies. Swamp red currants are used for the same things. Native black currants also can be used, but not everyone likes their flavor.

Currants, at least black ones, also have medicinal uses. Herbalists believe they purify the blood, restore the nervous system, and help in anemia and malnutrition, and are full of vitamins. Some also say that the wine of black currants is a valuable medicine. It is good for colds and bronchitis. How good it really is, you will have to discover through personal research.

Making Currant Wine

Wash two quarts of black currants. Crush them into a plastic pail. Pour one gallon of boiling water over them. Allow it to cool to room temperature.

Add three pounds of sugar, the juice of one lemon, and a package of wine yeast. Cover with a cheesecloth.

Stir the mixture every day with a wooden stick for seven days. Strain the must into a fermentation jug and water-seal it. Allow it to ferment (about six weeks).

Rack the wine into an aging vessel to age and clear. It should be ready to drink in one year.

Since currants contain much pectin, some recipes may call for a depectinizer to be added so the wine will clear.

GOOSEBERRIES

Gooseberry bushes are similar to currant bushes, except that nearly all gooseberry bushes are thorny, and the gooseberry fruits are sometimes quite prickly. There are a half dozen species growing wild in the northeastern United States. They tend to grow a littler farther south than currants and also are found in drier places.

A couple of species, like the northern gooseberry, *Ribes oxy-*

acanthoides, and *Ribes hirtellum*, are found in wet woods in Canada and the northern parts of the northernmost states.

Others, such as the Missouri gooseberry, grow farther south and over a wider range. These are often found in upland forests and can be quite abundant.

The gooseberry with perhaps the widest range is the dogberry or prickly gooseberry (*Ribes cynosbati*). It grows from Quebec to northern Minnesota and south to North Carolina and Oklahoma. It is widespread in moist woods within its range. There is usually little ground cover, making the going easy for the gooseberry picker.

Easy, that is until you get down to picking. The dogberry fruit is nearly always covered with weak but rather sharp spines, making picking them very hazardous to your fingers. In fact, the amount of jabbing you can stand is a limiting factor on how many you can pick.

The dogberry is the only member of the currant and gooseberry group to grow in many places. So if one bush is found other ones can be spotted fairly easily. You can often walk from gooseberry bush to gooseberry bush without interruption, though they may be fifty yards apart.

While walking through a moist maple forest one July day, I spotted some ripening dogberries along the trail. I had been fishing a trout stream a half mile through the woods from my car. As I approached my car in the parking area, there they were! I stopped to look around and found more bushes. After dumping my fishing equipment in the car, I scrounged up a plastic bag (always carry plastic bags in your car for opportunities like this) and started picking.

I picked only ripe ones, the ripest I could find. Some bushes were loaded with them, others were empty. Some appeared to have been stripped by animals—even the leaves and twigs were gone.

Since there was little undergrowth in that forest, I could see the gooseberries from a great distance. Their growth habit is distinctive. I picked ripe ones until my fingers could stand no more and left many green ones.

The gooseberry has less-noticed, economic importance. It is responsible for propagating white pine blister rust, which severely injures white pine trees. Blister rust is a parasitic fungus that lives one generation in the white pine, the next generation in gooseberry

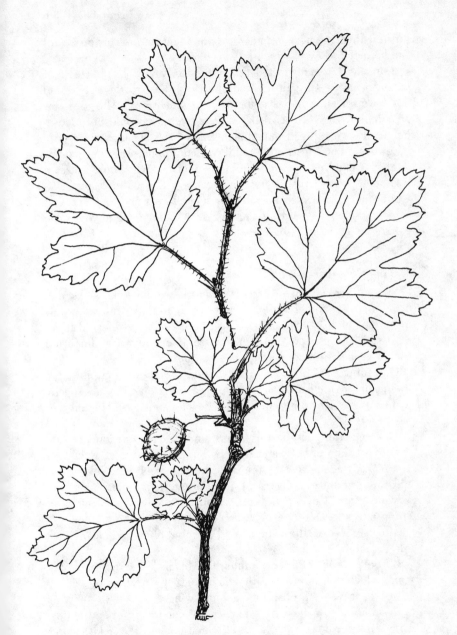

Prickly gooseberry or dogberry; *Ribes cynosbati*

bushes, then the next in the white pine, and so on. This distresses
the lumber industry, which loses tree crops.

Someone once suggested that the easy way to kill blister rust
would be to destroy all the gooseberry bushes, so the rust would
not have an alternate host for its next generation. The idea was
abandoned when it was realized what a task it would be. Gooseberries are widespread and found in many types of habitats. It would
be impossible to destroy them all without killing other vegetation.

That is good news for the home winemaker who could not care
less about blister rust. Gooseberries are a fine natural crop, like
white pine, and are appreciated by winemakers and foragers. Get
some gooseberries, and add another outstanding wine to your wine
cellar.

Making Gooseberry Wine

Many gooseberry wines are listed in the winemaking books, one
claiming to be one of the best white wines around. It is rather low
in tannin, high in acid and pectin. The gooseberry referred to, of
course, is the garden gooseberry, a commercial variety imported
from Europe. But any wild species can be used.

One thing to note about the gooseberry recipes is that not all of
them call for ripe fruit, some call for green ones, and others specify
half-ripe ones. The different stages of development result in different
flavored wines.

The recipe for gooseberries is very similar to the one for currants.

Pour a gallon of hot water over two quarts crushed gooseberries
in a plastic pail. When the temperature has dropped to lukewarm,
add three pounds of sugar, the juice of one lemon and a package
of wine yeast. Cover with cheesecloth. Stir daily for eight days.
Strain into a fermentation bottle and water-seal.

After six weeks, the wine should stop bubbling and clear. Rack
into an aging vessel.

Bottle the wine after seven months. This makes a very pale pink
wine, which will improve with aging. If green or semi-ripe berries
are used, it would probably be a white wine.

In addition to wines, gooseberries are good for pies and jellies.
They can be eaten raw as well, although eating the prickly gooseberry is indeed a delicate task.

RASPBERRIES

The common raspberry is found over a wide area across the south of Canada and in the northern United States. It is found in forests, pastures, waste areas, and roadsides. In some areas it is extremely abundant.

The common raspberry (*Rubus strigosus*) should not be confused with the cultivated raspberry from Europe, which has larger berries. The wild one has smaller, better tasting berries.

Found in patches, raspberries are grown on erect, arching, bristly canes, one-half to one meter tall, The leaves are compound, with

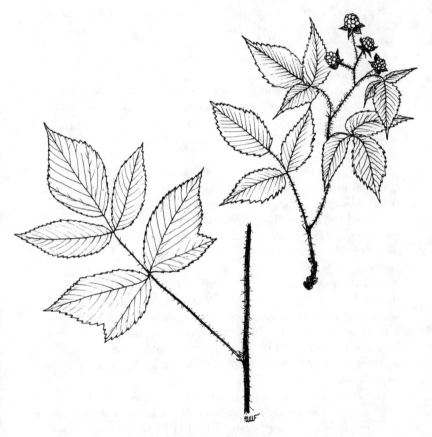

Wild raspberry; *Rubus strigosus*

three leaflets each. The flowers appear in clusters in June and blooms are produced over several weeks. The berries are ripe in July.

In shady areas, like woods, few fruits may be produced. But in an open meadow exposed to the full sun, large crops may be produced.

Each cane of the raspberry lives two years. The first year it emerges from the extensive underground root system of the patch and produces only leaves. The second year it produces flowers and fruits, after which it dies. Meanwhile the roots send up more canes. An entire patch of raspberries may have developed from a single seed.

Raspberries are ready to pick in the hottest part of the summer. Pick them morning or evening to avoid the heat. Watch where you step in the berry patch. The canes without fruits should not be trampled as they are needed for next year. Small animals may also be underfoot in a thick raspberry patch.

Many people who have eaten wild raspberries agree that this is the tastiest berry in nature's supermarket. Raspberries are used on shortcakes and in pies and jellies. They are best eaten raw, but when supply exceeds immediate demand, they can be frozen or made into wine.

Related species of raspberries can also be used for wine. The common black raspberry, or blackcap, can be found further south than other raspberries. Their fruits are similar, since they are both hollow when picked. But black raspberries are black when ripe and red when green or unripe. The black raspberry has a flavor all its own, which is as good as that of the red raspberry. It should make an excellent wine.

Two other raspberry species, Arctic raspberry (*Rubus acaulis*) and the dwarf raspberry (*Rubus pubescens*), are found mostly in Canada and in spruce bogs in the northernmost parts of the United States. The Arctic raspberry produces many fruits per cane, the dwarf raspberry only a few. Both species are unavailable to most people, and in the case of the dwarf raspberry, it would be difficult to find enough to make wine.

The thimbleberry, another raspberry of the north, is found in large areas of the western mountains, in the Black Hills, and grows in a limited area of northeastern United States ranging from Ontario's Bruce Peninsula in Lake Huron, around both sides of Lake

Superior to Minnesota. It is particularly abundant and grows large and profusely within a few miles of Lake Superior. Farther away from this area, the colonies of thimbleberry seem to be sickly.

Thimbleberries can be identified by their large, maple-like leaves, white-petaled flowers, smooth stems, and large pink fruits. The fruits resemble large raspberries and taste extremely tart. Residents of Michigan's Upper Peninsula make jams, jellies, and pies from thimbleberries.

Look for thimbleberries in August near the Lake Superior shore. They grow everywhere in the woods and can very often be seen in patches along roadsides.

The raspberry tribe is a fine producer of food, whether as dessert shortcake or dessert wine. Raspberries and black raspberries can be found in many areas in abundance for those who only want to make wine from their neighborhood. The other three species are in limited areas, available only to winemakers who are willing to go some distance for exotic homemade wine or for those who are lucky enough to live near them. Pick a batch of raspberries next season and have a real raspberry-tasting wine.

Making Raspberry Wine

Making wine sometimes seems like such a waste of the flavor of fresh raspberries. Fortunately, some of the flavor gets through. Most winemaking books require far more raspberries for their recipes than are used in the following one. This recipe is similar to blackberry wine recipes because blackberries and raspberries are both members of the genus *Rubus*.

Mash one or two quarts of raspberries in a pail. Add three pounds of sugar and mix together well.

Pour a gallon of boiling water over this. Let cool to room temperature and add the wine yeast. Cover with cheesecloth and let stand for seven to ten days, stirring daily.

Strain into a fermentation jug and water-seal. Allow it to work for several months. When it clears, bottle and age for a year. Raspberries produce a good dessert wine.

BLACKBERRIES AND DEWBERRIES

Every Labor Day for many years, my family went "up north" to

Wisconsin's Northwoods to pick blackberries. This was an end-of-summer tradition, trying to gather enough blackberries from the clearings and roadsides to freeze for winter pies.

We still go there to pick berries, but since the blackberries have declined, we now pick dewberries, a close relative of the blackberries.

Blackberries and dewberries are related to the raspberry tribe, being classed in the same genus. Unlike raspberries, the fruits are solid and firm when picked. The canes are often covered with sharp spines or thorns. The ripening season is usually somewhat later than for raspberries.

Blackberries and dewberries are found in a great many species, as well as hybrids. It can be difficult even for experts to tell them apart. They may grow tall arching canes over seven feet tall or small

Blackberry; *Rubus allegheniensis*

ones trailing along the ground. The fruits can be one-fourth to one inch long. They sometimes grow in peat bogs, but most species seem to prefer dry ground. The flavor from each species of berry is somewhat different.

The main difference between blackberries and dewberries is size. Blackberry canes are tall and erect, while dewberries are short and trailing. Blackberries produce cylindrical fruits an inch long; dewberries produce smaller, often round, fruit. Blackberries are often sweeter tasting than dewberries. Dewberries ripen sometimes weeks earlier than blackberries growing in the same neighborhood.

Dewberries are more dependable than blackberries. Blackberries produce the most fruit if the patch is relatively new. After that, the patch may grow profusely but never flower or fruit. Dewberries seem to be able to fruit consistently year after year, barring severe drought.

For the purpose of recipes, blackberries and dewberries are interchangeable. Blackberries are larger, so they are easier to pick. Blackberries may be sweeter, so taste them before picking to see if the berry has the flavor you seek.

Blackberries and dewberries are found in many parts of the country. At least one and probably a number of species can be found near most home winemakers. Look for them along bulldozed dirt roads, cut over forests, pine barrens, and dry fields. They are easiest to spot in May and June when their large white flowers are conspicuous from a distance. Then return in July and check on their progress. In the north, they may not ripen until nearly September.

Pick them on a dry, preferably a warm and sunny, day. Do not wear shorts into the blackberry or dewberry patch, unless you carry a lot of band-aids along. The spines on the bushes are just waiting to grab unsuspecting berry pickers. Wear old blue jeans.

Blackberry jam can be made easily and is good if you do not mind biting into seeds. Blackberry jelly is preferable since it is minus seeds. Blackberry cobbler is still another recipe. In the South, dewberry pie is made. Blackberry juice and a tea made from blackberry leaves have been used to cure diarrhea.

Blackberry and dewberry wine is actually a great many wines, since each species of berry has a noticeably different taste. The end product of each will be slightly different. If two or more species are mixed, even more kinds of wine can be made.

Making Blackberry and Dewberry Wine

Wash the berries and discard the green and semi-ripe ones. Mash up the berries (about three pints) in a pail. They should be juicy if possible, but in a drought year, they may be dry. Add three pounds of sugar and mix together. Pour a gallon of boiling water over the berries and sugar and stir. Let it sit until it is at room temperature, then add wine yeast and mix well. Cover with cheesecloth and let work for seven days, stirring daily. Then strain into a fermentation vessel and water-seal. This will work and bubble for about six months, maybe longer. Then siphon into an aging vessel and age for a year before bottling. It should clear by itself and produce a deep red wine, which may lose some color if exposed to too much light.

The consensus of home winedrinkers (who are more numerous than home winemakers) is that this is a hearty wine which is good with beef. It is a favorite with deer hunters, who brave cold November weather and like a little antifreeze, and with ice fishermen, who brave even worse weather.

Other blackberry wine recipes in winemaking books assume the use of cultivated blackberries, but any blackberries or dewberries will do. Most require the use of more blackberries than this recipe, but I like to stress smaller quantities of wine and more varieties.

Other recipes also call for other ingredients. One calls for adding mulberries and sloes, more of them than blackberries. This would hardly be called blackberry wine. Another recipe is called blackberry honey wine and calls for adding honey, cinnamon, and cloves.

So when the dog days of August are upon us, go out and get some blackberries or dewberries. They are easy to find and easy to pick. Then make some wine from a simple recipe, and put it away to drive away the chills on a cold winter day.

ROSE HIPS

Roses are the flowers of romance. Many a heart has been swayed by a bouquet of long-stemmed roses. Poets and writers make much of the beauty of the rose. It seems to reach man's standard of floral beauty more than any other flower.

Thousands of varieties of roses are cultivated, and new ones appear on the market each year. Some people grow roses as a hobby.

Cultivated roses were developed from wild ones. The double-flowered, red, yellow, white, or lavender-blue roses all descended from wild species with five pink petals per flower. There are dozens of species of wild roses around the world.

In the northeastern United States there are about twenty species. Some are native to the area and widespread. Others are European species, whose seeds escaped from cultivated plants and went wild. These are more localized in range.

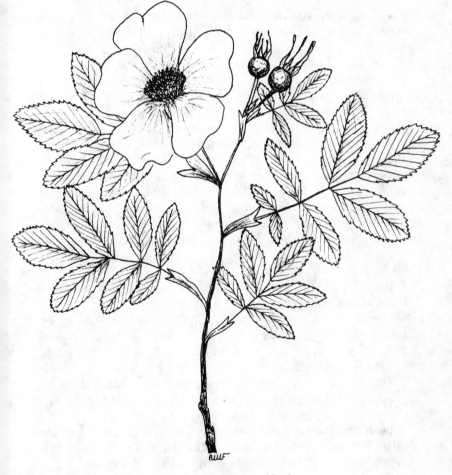

Smooth wild rose; *Rosa blanda*

Some native species are found along streams and in swamps, such as the Swamp Rose (*Rosa palustris*). Others include the Meadow Rose (*Rosa blanda*) and the Pasture Rose (*Rosa carolina*) found in meadows and along forest edges, roadsides, and railroad tracks. There is also the Prairie Wild Rose (*Rosa arkansana*) that grows in dry areas. Some escaped wild roses also do well in dry places, especially disturbed ones.

Wild roses bloom from May to July, depending on locale, though they often bloom on Lake Superior beaches in the middle of August. Their fragrance attracts bees from great distances, and they are readily pollinated. The seeds and fruit develop slowly during the summer.

The fruit is called a rose hip. It consists of part of the flower receptacle that grows up around the seeds, enclosing them. It is green all summer, turns orange late in August or September, then red in October. They are ready to pick when they are red.

Rose hips are known for their abundance of vitamin C. Humans, monkeys, and guinea pigs are the only creatures that cannot make their own vitamin C and must ingest it. Vitamin C is needed to maintain the body's collagen levels. (Collagen is the glue that holds cells together.) It is needed for ligaments, gum tissues, and blood vessel walls. It is needed for normal healing and resistance to infection. (Some people allege it prevents colds if taken in massive doses.) Rose hips have a higher concentration of vitamin C than oranges. Rose hips from cultivated roses have a lower vitamin C content than wild ones, and some wild species have more vitamin C than others. The vitamin C tablets sold in health food stores are often made from rose hips.

During World War II, England, Norway, and Sweden suffered from a vitamin C shortage, since little citrus fruit could be convoyed past the submarines. Studies made of native plants showed rose hips to have the highest vitamin C concentration. So the civilian population scoured the rose gardens, hedgerows, and meadows for both wild and cultivated rose hips. They gathered thousands of pounds and used them to make teas and soups.

Rose hips also contain other vitamins, A, B_1, B_2, E, K, P, niacin, calcium, phosphorus, and iron. Sort of like reading the back of a cereal box, except they come by all these nutrients naturally!

Rose hips were used as a food by the ancient Greeks, a thousand years before Christ. They recognized the health-giving qualities of this fruit without having heard of vitamins.

In addition to rose hip teas and soups, a very delicious jam can be made from rose hips. Also a wine can be produced. Some Germans consider rose hip wine second only to grape wine.

Look for wild rose bushes early in the summer, when large patches are readily discernible by their pink blooms. Then go back and look for them in October. Or wait until November, December, or January to pick rose hips. The vegetation will be dead, but the hips will persist on the plants. The bright red hips will be quite visible in the winter sunshine. As the winter progresses they tend to dry and wrinkle but they can still be used. Birds tend to get their share as the winter progresses, also, so pick early.

Gathering rose hips in a good patch will take only a couple of hours. A bush may be over one meter tall and contain a hundred rose hips. Pick large hips if possible, as they fill the collecting bag faster and have more vitamin C. Some hips may be a half a centimeter in diameter, others almost two and a half centimeters.

Making Rose Hip Wine

Gather three and a half pounds of rose hips and inspect for rejects. Cut the ends off them. This is an easy, but very tedious job. Then cut them in half. For other rose hip recipes, the seeds must be removed, but not for wine.

Pour a gallon of boiling water over the rose hips in a plastic pail. This will destroy some of the vitamins, but not all of them. Add three pounds of sugar. When cool, add a package of wine yeast and cover with cheesecloth. Let it stand and stir daily for a week. Strain the must into a fermentation jug and water-seal. Allow it to ferment for about six weeks. Then siphon the liquid into an aging jug. Three months later, to help the wine clear, siphon it into another aging vessel. For best results, let it age a minimum of two years.

My father made rose hip wine, full of high hopes. After a few months of aging, when he thought it would be ready, he tried it. It was horrible, but he put some bottles away anyway. After two years, when he was looking for spare wine bottles, he decided to throw out the rose hip wine and put the bottles to better use. He gave the rose hip wine one last chance. It was superb! He gave some to my mother, who was suffering from a cold virus. She thought it was delicious, and next day all symptoms of her cold were gone. She is now convinced that rose hip wine is a cold cure.

WILD APPLES

Apple trees and apple orchards are seen throughout the northern United States. In suitable localities, apples have become a major industry. Apples are processed and sold commercially as dessert apples, applesauce, apple butter, apple jelly, apple cider, and as the main ingredient in "mom's apple pie." Numerous other recipes are made from apples, mostly from the cultivated varieties. The tree species commonly known as apple is not native to the United States, but imported from Europe.

The first true apples are believed to have been developed in the Caucasus Mountains, as hybrids between European and Asiatic crab apples. Man began cultivating them in ancient times and carried the seeds to Europe.

The first European colonists to migrate to America found the wild American crab apples not to their liking and imported apple seeds. Apple seedlings or cuttings would have been unlikely to survive the trip, so the first American apples were seed-grown.

Apples are highly variable and each tree grown from seed is likely to be quite different from its neighbor. That is why all commercial apple varieties are grown by grafting twigs of existing trees onto roots grown from seed. The top of the seedling is not permitted to grow, in favor of the known variety. Most apple seedlings will not provide fruit of good eating quality anyway.

Apple orchards were grown from seed in America until the end of the eighteenth century. By then many orchards were being planted from grafted cuttings. The grafted trees were well suited to the soil and climate and were spread across the country. They managed to spread beyond the orchards into fence rows, pastures, and roadsides. The apples rotted, and the seeds sprouted. Now there are many areas with wild, seed-grown populations of apples. Their qualities may not be the best, but they work very well for wine.

A large wild apple population grows on a hillside in an old pasture

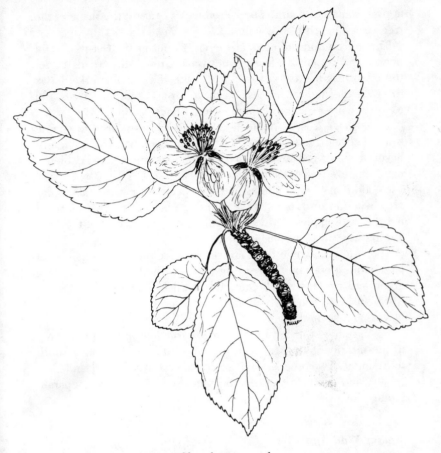

Wild apple; *Pyrus malus*

near where I live. There are many seedlings and immature trees
not yet old enough to bear fruit, located mostly downhill of the adult
trees. They probably got there by kids eating the apples and giving
the cores a toss. The adult trees display a wide variety of characteristics.

Some of these apple trees are highly resistant to insects and disease, others are not. Some bloom early, some late. Some have apples
that are bright red when they are ripe, others are nearly green when
ripe. Some are quite tart, others sweet. Many have very small

apples, some quite large ones. Productivity varies; the shape of the tree varies—each tree is unique.

This hillside on the edge of the city is out of sight of roads and houses and requires a five-minute walk through the woods to get there, so it is harvested very little. With the aid of a forked stick to reach the highest apples, I can go around sampling trees and gather a winter's supply of apples in an hour.

If you have a large population of wild apples nearby to choose from, go from tree to tree and taste them. Each tree has a different flavored apple. The tart ones make better wine and cider. Try blending a mixture of flavors for your wine.

In addition to wild apples, several species of native crab apples grow wild in varous parts of the country. Some of them have formed hybrids with apples. Most crab apples are very small, but they can also be used for wine, using the apple recipe.

The wild crab apple trees are similar to apple trees, small, with large white petals on their spring flowers. The fruits in the fall are green and two and a half centimeters thick. Different species are distinguished from each other by technical differences in their leaves, and several species are found in the same areas.

For instance, the Iowa Crabapple (*Pyrus iowenus*) is found only in the interior, from Michigan west to southern Minnesota, south to Arkansas. Two other species are found east to New York and New Jersey, and south to Georgia. Still another species has a separate range, along the West Coast.

Making Wild Apple Wine

Wild apples are generally preferred over crab apples for wine-making because of their size. Pick six pounds of apples. This can take some time if they are very small. Inspect each one for worms and wash them. Core and quarter them and run them through a food chopper. Put the chopped apples in the pail and pour a gallon of boiling water over them. Add three pounds sugar and stir. Thinly peel a lemon and put the peelings in a small sauce pan with one-half cup water. Boil for ten minutes and pour peels and water into apple mixture. Add the juice of the peeled lemon and stir.

When cooled to room temperature, add a package of wine yeast. Cover with cheesecloth and stir daily for seven days. Strain the must into a fermentation jug and water-seal. Fermentation will subside in about six weeks. Siphon the wine into an aging jug, leaving the residue. Age in the jug for one year, then pour into wine bottles or drink.

This makes a good white wine, especially if tart and sweet apples were mixed together.

MOUNTAIN ASH

The mountain ash, a member of the rose family, may be most familiar as a small backyard or boulevard tree. It has leaves that are compound, with eight or ten leaflets on each leaf stem, or rachis. It is most conspicuous for the large clusters of bright orange berries that develop in late summer and remain on the tree well into winter.

It is also known as a wild tree. About a hundred species of mountain ash, in the genus *Sorbus*, are known worldwide. Two species grow wild in the northeastern United States, and more in the West. Others come from Europe and Asia.

The American mountain ash (*Sorbus americana*) is a small tree up to nine meters tall. It forms thick clusters of flowers in July. The fruits, only half a centimeter in diameter, are bright red when they are ripe in late August. This species is common in the evergreen forest areas of Canada, reaching south into the Great Lakes area, and along the mountains to North Carolina.

The other native mountain ash (*Sorbus decora*) is a somewhat larger tree with larger fruits. Otherwise it looks generally the same. It is found in woods, on slopes, and along shores. This mountain ash is somewhat more wildly ranging than the American mountain ash but is still primarily a northern tree. Found from the southwest coast of Greenland, through Labrador, across Canada to southeast Manitoba, it ranges southward to western Massachusetts, northern Ohio and Indiana, and Wisconsin. It is quite common along the north shore of Lake Superior where, in the fall, the bright red fruit is conspicuous at quite a distance.

If the berries of the wild mountain ash can be found, try them in a wine. Try using the orange fruits of the cultivated mountain ash, if you can get them away from the birds. Songbirds love the cultivated variety of berries. The wild ones are readily eaten by sharptail grouse, blue grouse, and assorted ptarmigans. In the West, mountain ash berries have been used since pioneer days in jams and jellies. They were an important source of food for Indians. Now for the inventive winemaker, they can also be an important source of wine.

Making Wild Mountain Ash Wine

I have not tried any mountain ash wine, because I have not been near any wild trees at harvest time. However, I have found a recipe that is said to make an excellent mountain ash wine.

First, collect the berries. Since they ripen late and unripe ones are pretty sour, wait to collect them until after a frost. They will be gathered in clusters. Field-grown trees may have branches and fruit

Mountain ash; *Sorbus decora*

reaching near enough to the ground to reach by hand. Forest specimens may not have any within reach, so a forked stick or long pole may be needed to shake them loose. If the tree is small, try shaking it. It won't hurt the fruits if they hit the ground.

Inspect and wash five pounds of the berries. Crush them in a plastic pail and pour a gallon of boiling water over them. Add three and a half pounds of sugar and the juice of one lemon. Mix well and let cool to room temperature. Add wine yeast and cover with cheesecloth. Stir daily for seven days.

Strain into a fermentation jug and water-seal. Allow to ferment until the bubbles cease. This could take from six weeks to six months. Then siphon liquid into an aging vessel. Sample the wine. Being a fruit wine, it will require six months to a year of aging before it can be bottled and drunk.

JUNEBERRIES

Juneberries are noticed most easily early in the spring. Their long-petaled, white flowers grow in clusters that are in full bloom before most trees have opened their buds. The early spring wildflowers have hardly begun before the juneberry bushes adorn themselves with white. In the East, they acquired the name shadbush because they bloomed at the time the shad run upstream to spawn. In other areas, they are called serviceberries.

Juneberries are usually shrubs or small trees. Some places in the east, they can reach ten to fifteen meters tall, but usually they are much smaller. There are about eight or ten species in the northeastern United States (all in the genus *Amelanchier*), but one or another species of juneberry can be found throughout much of the United States and southern Canada.

Most species of juneberry are very similar, having been frequently crossbred, but there are some obvious differences. Different species have berries with different flavors, which is very important in winemaking. Most kinds bear flowers and fruits heavily, but one (*Amelanchier bartramiana*) bears only solitary flowers and relatively few. Since it is a northern shrub of bog edges, it is not likely to be found by juneberry pickers.

Different species also have different blooming seasons. Some do not blossom until June, with fruit ripening in August. Others blossom in April or May, with ripe fruit in June or early July.

Juneberries are found in a variety of habitats, including forest edges, thickets, and streambanks. I have picked them in an open jack oak forest in northern Wisconsin, where the bushes were one to three meters tall. The fruits were ripe in early July, so this was an early species (probably *Amelanchier laevis*).

Juneberries ripen over several weeks. Ripe ones, half ripe ones, and green ones can be found on the same bush. Birds and other animals frequently eat ripe juneberries.

Juneberries are used as a sauce and in pies and muffins. They can be canned, frozen, or made into cider. The Indians mixed dried juneberries with pemmican. The Chippewas routinely packed juneberries on their journeys.

Learn to recognize juneberry bushes by their masses of white flowers in the spring. Since they are members of the rose family, the flowers have five petals, usually long ones, and may be several centimeters across. Some of the fruits will be red when ripe, others a dark purple. Some of the small leaves will turn yellow by berry season, making juneberry bushes easier to spot from a distance.

Juneberries are so delicious raw you will find yourself sampling them from time to time while you are picking them. They are very sweet and sugary, with a flavor all their own. If you plan to make wine, be sure to save three pints of juneberries from the sampling process.

Making Juneberry Wine

Go over the juneberries and discard all bird-eaten ones. Then wash the berries thoroughly. Mash them up in the plastic pail and pour a gallon of boiling water over them. Add three pounds of sugar. Stir. When the mixture is at room temperature, add the wine yeast. Cover with cheesecloth and let it work in a warm place for seven days, stirring daily. Strain and pour into a fermentation jug and water-seal. When the bubbling has subsided, siphon out into wine bottles. No aging is necessary.

This process makes a dry red wine, a suitable accompaniment for spaghetti or steaks. This is one wine that is not only started in summer, it is ready to drink in summer. Whether the berries are

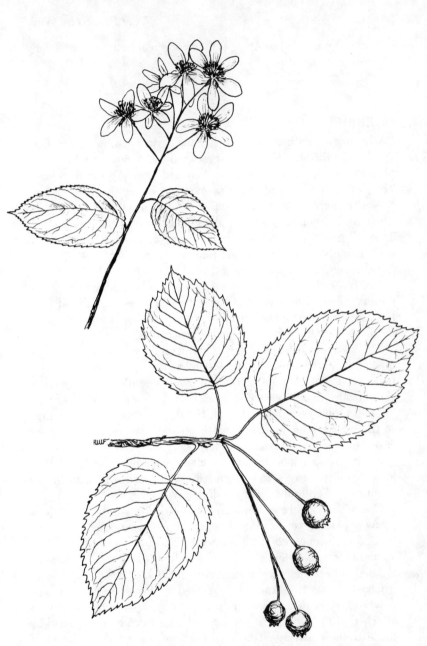

Smooth Juneberry; *Amelanchier laevis*

picked in June, July, or August, they are a real treat no matter how they are consumed.

CHERRIES

Cherries are cultivated in much of the eastern United States. One species of cultivated cherries has escaped and is now found in many places as a wild tree, called the Mazzard cherry (*Prunus avium*). The fruit they produce is often as good as some cultivated varieties.

Native cherry trees are also found over much of the United States. Their fruit is not as good, but all cherries can be made into wine. They all produce white flowers in spring, and red or nearly black fruits in midsummer. Four wide-ranging cherries are black cherries, pin cherries, choke cherries, and sand cherries.

The black cherry grows on a very large tree; reaching twenty-five meters tall it is the largest of the native cherries. It is found from Nova Scotia to North Dakota and south to Texas and Florida growing in forests and along forest edges and roadsides.

The wood of the black cherry is excellent for cabinet making. The quality of the wood is such that many of the very large trees have been cut down for lumber. It is said that Daniel Boone, in his spare time, made several black cherry caskets, giving away all but one.

Field-grown trees are common, but do not grow straight and tall so they make poor lumber. That is all right, as their cherries are easier to reach come harvest time.

Black cherries look much like choke cherries. The trees have longer-pointed leaves and rough bark. They form ripe fruit in late August and September that is edible raw.

Choke cherries are wide-ranging small trees or shrubs. They grow in many places, wet or dry. They can be found on dunes, in rocks, in mud or swampy edges. They seem to sprout everywhere. They are found from Newfoundland to Saskatchewan and south to Kansas. Related varieties also grow in western United States.

Choke cherry trees can be recognized in May when they produce flower clusters that appear from a distance to be white cylinders attached to the twigs. Then in late July, they can be recognized by the extremely astringent taste of the ripe fruit. The old tale that anyone eating choke cherries will choke is not literally true, but if

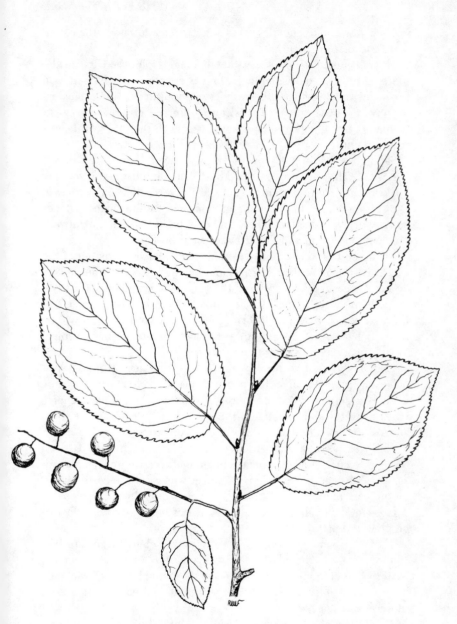

Choke cherry; *Prunus virginiana*

you eat raw choke cherries, you might prefer to choke than keep that taste in your mouth.

The pin cherry tree is somewhat taller and is found across Canada, south to Indiana and Colorado. Flowers appear in April or May in small clusters directly off the twig, as opposed to cylindrical clusters on separate little stems. Fruits form from the flowers in August. Instead of being dark red or almost black as in the other wild cherries, pin cherries are a light red color and taste rather sour.

Sand cherries do not grow on trees, but very low shrubs only a meter tall. They are prostrate and branch along the ground, sending up leafy and fruiting stems. There are several different varieties, found from Maine to Wyoming growing mostly in isolated patches on very dry, sterile sand. They can be found in acid, glacial outwash sands of Wisconsin and Great Lakes sand beaches.

At the end of May or early June flowers appear singly out of the leaf axils, but one plant can produce many flowers. If the flowers do not freeze in a late frost and the bees pollinate them, fruits will form. If the weather is dry, the fruits will be dry and wrinkled. If the weather is wet enough, firm, juicy, black sand cherries will be ready to harvest in July and August. Sand cherries are more subject to the vagaries of weather than most fruits.

Cherries in general have been used for a variety of things. Appalachian pioneers invented a drink called a "cherry bounce" by using black cherry juice in brandy. The Indians boiled black cherry twigs in water and sweetened the drink in maple sugar. Cherries are used to make jellies, pies, soup, juice, and wine.

Cherries also have been used as medicine. They have been thought to cure tension, stomach inflammations, rheumatism, headaches, and head colds. Cherry gum, a sticky substance produced by the bark of the tree, dissolved in wine is thought to cure coughs. A large intake of cherries or cherry juice is believed to be effective on gout and arthritis.

This is all very curious since cherries and cherry trees are poisonous. In fact, the black cherry is a hazard to livestock in the eastern United States. The leaves contain so much cyanide that only a few ounces of leaves can kill a large animal. Wilted leaves are even more deadly.

All species of cherry contain some cyanide but will do no harm to humans at normal usage levels. The roots, the bark, the leaves, and even the pits contain levels of cyanide. The cherry pulp also contains a minor amount of cyanide. Black cherry is the most dangerous, pin cherry the least. My grandmother used to make cherry pickles, cucumbers soaked in pin cherry leaves. Choke cherry leaves were sometimes used, but if she had known what was in them, she might have reconsidered. They were tasty though and didn't hurt anybody.

Making Wild Cherry Wine

First, get the cherries. Choke cherries are easiest to find, as they are abundant, widespread, and the cherries can be quickly stripped off their stems. Black cherries may be higher up the trees, otherwise they are easy to get and have more juice. Sand cherries, in a good year, can be carefully stripped off their branches, and they are always easy to reach. Pin cherries, the small red ones, will take longer to pick and are harder to reach.

Mash two quarts of fresh, juicy cherries in a plastic pail. Pick out a dozen cherry pits, crush them, and throw them back in the pail. Pour a gallon of boiling water over them. Mix in three pounds of sugar. When at room temperature, add the wine yeast. Cover with cheesecloth and let work for eight days, stirring daily. Strain into a fermentation jug and water-seal. Allow to ferment to completion. Then siphon into an aging vessel and allow to age at least one year before drinking.

An alternative recipe for black cherry wine calls for five pounds of cherries and three and a half pounds of sugar. Use the same procedure as above. This produces a sweeter wine.

It is essential to age this wine. Choke cherry wine must be aged longer than the rest, perhaps two years. Its astringency goes right through to the new wine. A winemaker tasting choke cherry wine right out of the fermentation jug will be inclined to throw out the winemaking equipment. With age however, it comes around.

WILD PLUMS

When I was a boy, there was a wild plum thicket in our neighborhood. It was less than a hundred feet square, but it was a very absorbing place to play. In spring, the numerous white blooms

covered the thorny branches. During the summer, there were regular neighborhood plum fights, with green plums as the weapons.
Green plums were softer and smoother than rocks, so there were
no casualties.

In late August, the green plums would turn yellow, then red.
They would fall off the trees when they got too ripe. They had a
tasty pulp, but a very astringent skin.

This species was the American plum (*Prunus americana*). (Plums
are in the same genus as cherries.) The American plum is the most
common and widespread of wild plums, found from Connecticut to
Montana and south into Mexico. It is a small, rather twisted, thorny
tree or shrub growing in thickets, along roadsides, and on riverbanks. The flowers have a distinctive fragrance when they are blos-
soming in April or May.

The American plum is so adaptable that 300 cultivated varieties
have been derived from it, though cultivated varieties have been
developed from other plums.

Another rather widespread species is the Canada plum (*Prunus
nigra*), which has larger and tastier fruits than the American plum.
Canada plums are not astringent like American plums, and can be
eaten in large quantities raw. The Canada plum has larger flowers,
and the fruits ripen earlier, usually in August. It is found in thickets
and along forest edges, from Quebec to Manitoba and south to Ohio
and Iowa. It occurs in scattered patches and localities throughout
its range.

When Jacques Cartier, the French explorer, arrived in Canada
in 1535, he landed on an island in the St. Lawrence that was covered
with Canada plums. He was amazed at the abundance and picked
many of them. Now, varieties of Canada plums are cultivated in
French Canada.

Wild plums are found throughout the eastern United States, but
still may not be available to everyone. Most kinds have limited
ranges. The California plum (*Prunus subcordata*) is found only in
northern California and southern Oregon, for example. Even more
limited in range is the Beach plum (*Prunus maritima*). Found from
New Brunswick to Virginia, this plum grows along Atlantic beaches
and occasionally as far as twenty miles inland. It is sometimes harvested for the market. The Chicksaw plum (*Prunus angustifolia*) is
found from New Jersey and Indiana southward, in woods and thick-

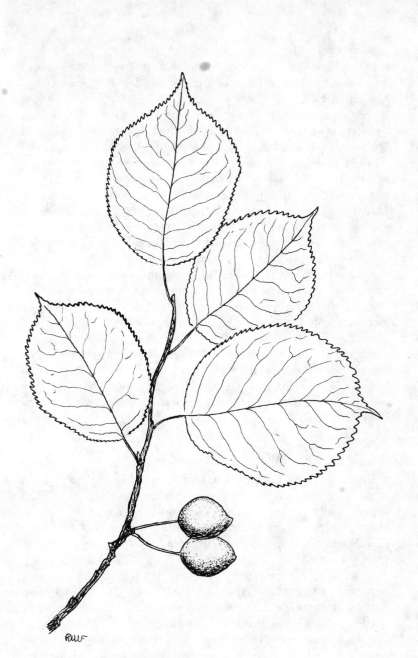

Wild plum; *Prunus americana*

ets. The Hortulan plum (*Prunus hortulana*) is restricted to moist woods and thickets in the region of the middle Mississippi valley. It is rather rare.

One more plum, the Wild Goose plum (*Prunus munsoniana*) has an interesting history. It is found in thickets from Kentucky and Missouri southward. In the 1830s a man in Nashville, Tennessee, shot a wild goose that had a plum pit in its craw. He planted the pit, and it fruited three years later. The plum tree was turned over to a nurseryman, who proceeded to develop new varieties from it. This species is most common in the Mississippi River floodplains.

The places to look for wild plums are roadsides, thickets, and moist forest edges. Their twisted thorny branches are often major components of the thicket.

With practice, plum bushes can be recognized in winter by their shape and thorns. In spring, the flowers and fragrance are distinctive. In August and September, ripe plums are somewhat similar to cherries, but plums are larger. Plum pits are flat and have a "plummy" flavor.

Picking plums for wine is easy because they are large and fill the pail quickly. They are also usually at a comfortable height, so no bending or stretching is required. If the trees produce at all, they produce in abundance. A few minutes of picking, once one has found the plums, is all it takes.

Making Wild Plum Wine

Crush two quarts of plums in a plastic pail. Pour three pounds of sugar over them. Add a gallon of boiling water and stir. When at room temperature, add the wine yeast. Cover with cheesecloth and stir daily for one week. Strain into a fermentation jug and waterseal. When bubbling has ceased, siphon into aging vessel. Wait a year, then bottle.

Plums are high in pectin, so it may be a good idea to add a depectinizer beforehand. If this isn't done, the wine may not clear readily. If the wine does not clear, siphon it into another aging vessel or use another clearing technique.

Plum wines, like cherry wines, must be aged for some time. American plum wine needs to be aged longer than other species. The astringency of the skins goes through to the wine, making it nearly undrinkable at first. With proper aging, all plums can be converted into excellent wines.

Some wine books list recipes for prune wines, damson wines, sloe wines, greengage wines, and apricot wines. These fruits are all close relatives of plums, and the various recipes can be used for wild plums.

In addition wild plums can be used for jellies, preserves, pies, pudding, or eaten raw.

WILD CRANBERRIES

Cranberries grow freely in bogs and swamps in the northern areas of the United States.

The Indians used cranberries in large quantities before whites ever arrived. In fact, it is one of the things the Indians taught the Pilgrims to use, which is why we eat cranberries at Thanksgiving. Because cranberries keep for a long time and were abundant in the Massachusetts area, many were shipped to England by early colonists.

It is only for the last hundred years or so that cranberries have been cultivated. The cultivation and harvest techniques are rather refined. They are grown in wet, boggy areas that can be flooded. As bogs are low places where frosts are possible in midsummer, care must be taken to avoid frosts. In cranberry-growing areas the television stations carry nighttime temperature forecasts for the bogs during the growing season.

Cranberries are not cultivated in many areas. Massachusetts and the Cap Cod area are the largest producers, closely followed by central and northern Wisconsin. These areas provide much of the nation's supply.

Cranberries are used for jelly, sauce, pie, muffins, pudding, ice cream, sherbert, cookies, and tarts. Euell Gibbons made cranberry glace, cranberry whip, and cranberry "mock cherry" pie.

The cranberry in cultivation is called *Vaccinium macrocarpon*. It is found in the wild in open bogs, swamps, and wet shores from Canada south to Illinois and North Carolina.

It is a low, delicate, creeping shrub. The leaves are small, elliptical, and leathery. Flowers do not occur until June and have four pink petals, turned straight back, and a long yellow "bill" of stamens.

The shape of the flowers gave cranberries their original name, craneberries.

The fruits turn red in October and will stay on the plants all winter. There may be many fruits per stem. A good locale may produce a good harvest of wild cranberries each fall.

Two other species of cranberries are found in the eastern United States, both generally farther north. One of these is the mountain cranberry (*Vaccinium vitis-idaea*). This is a matted shrub with erect branches. It is found all across Canada, barely reaching into northern New England and northern Minnesota. The mountain cranberry is

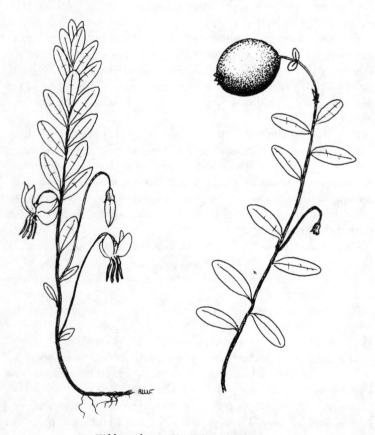

Wild cranberry; *Vaccinium macrocarpon*

considered a prime substitute for cultivated cranberries, better tasting in spring than fall. The berry is generally not edible until cooked, although bears love them.

When Henry David Thoreau went to Maine, he found that mountain cranberries were a favorite dessert. A highly prized larger form of this species is imported from Norway under the name "Lingonberries" and offered on pancakes in pancake shops.

The other species of cranberry is the small cranberry (*Vaccinium oxycoccos*). It is a small, creeping prostrate plant, generally found farther north than common cranberry. It grows in sphagnum bogs and wet, acid places from Labrador to Alaska and south to New Jersey, West Virginia, and Wisconsin. The small cranberry plant can be distinguished from others by the flowers and fruits on long stems at the tip of the plant. Common cranberries have fruits on long stems out of the leaf axils, and mountain cranberries have fruits on short stems at the tips of the branches.

With only one or a few fruits per plant each year, it takes longer to pick enough, but small cranberry plants can be quite abundant in bogs. I have found the small cranberry to be numerous in the bogs of northern Wisconsin, blooming in June and ready to harvest at hunting season.

Finding the cranberries will depend not only on living in the range of cranberries, but also on being able to find their habitants. Sphagnum bogs are quite common in the glaciated regions, but not common at all south of there. Look for sphagnum or generally wet, acid areas to find cranberries. They will be red, or turning red, in October and are easy to see against the dull greens and brown-reds of bog vegetation at that time of year.

Making Wild Cranberry Wine

The lovely cranberry wine is another claimant for the best of the non-grape wines. A similar species in Europe, called the billberry, has long been held in high esteem for wine. It is an excellent red wine, good not only by itself, but with other things, as shall be seen.

Cut up three pounds of washed cranberries. Use either a knife or a food chopper and coarsely chop them. Put them in a plastic pail with a pound of raisins and three pounds of sugar. Add a gallon of boiling water and stir. When at room temperature, add the wine yeast. Cover with cheesecloth and let ferment in the pail for two weeks, stirring daily. Strain into a fermentation jug and water-seal. At the end of fermentation, siphon into an aging jug. Age for a minimum of nine months before bottling and drinking.

When Christmas comes, the finished cranberry wine can be used in a holiday punch. Mix one and a half bottles of cranberry wine, one and a half large bottles of Seven Up soft drink, a six-ounce can of frozen lemonade mix, one or two oranges cut into slices, and a bottle of maraschino cherries and the juice. Mix this well and serve at parties.

Cranberry wine is also a good cooking wine. One day after watching Julia Child on *The French Chef*, we decided to try her recipe Coq au vin, chicken in red wine. Since she wasn't too particular about which red wine, we used cranberry. It worked wonderfully! The chicken, mushrooms, whole onions, and red wine were absolutely delicious over rice. When in need of a red wine for cooking, remember cranberry.

BLUEBERRIES AND HUCKLEBERRIES

Blueberries are closely related to cranberries, both being in the genus *Vaccinium*. However, blueberries are more numerous and widespread than cranberries. There are a dozen or more species in the eastern United States and another dozen on the West Coast. Some are found on the Atlantic and Gulf coastal plains, but they are more common northward.

Blueberries have long been a source of food for man. In the upper Great Lakes states, the common blueberry (*Vaccinium angustifolium*) was a very important source of food for the Indians. When Henry Schoolcraft visited the Namekagon River in northwest Wisconsin in 1831, he found the banks and surrounding area covered with berries. It was also covered with Indians, who had moved to the berrying grounds especially to gather blueberries. Some of the berries were eaten fresh, but most were spread out and dried for the winter.

The common blueberry is abundant in the acid sand plains and forests of Upper Michigan, Wisconsin, and Minnesota, but can be found as far south as Illinois. It is usually less than half a meter high, with small bell-shaped blooms appearing about the end of May and into June.

In the northern range, blueberries can suffer severely from late frosts. The bushes are frost resistant, but the flowers are not. A light frost during blooming season may destroy much of the crop growing in the open, sparing those in the shelter of trees. A hard frost can kill the entire crop of blueberries in an area.

Although blueberries are usually small shrubs, sometimes they are large. The Swamp blueberry (*Vaccinium corymbosum*) can grow as tall as five meters.

Low blueberry; *Vaccinium angustifolium*

In good years, blueberries can be gathered by the quarts. I once found a small but abundant patch of green blueberries. A week later, I returned to that spot early. After making sure the coast was clear (this is one berry that northern Wisconsin summer people do not ignore), I plunged into the woods, found the patch, and started picking. A buck deer, antlers in velvet, walked up to me, but did not interrupt my picking. Two more deer sprinted back and forth through the nearby woods, but I kept picking. That twenty square foot patch of bushes scarcely six inches high yielded almost two quarts of berries—an exceptional harvest.

Sometimes blueberries are found in patches, with many berries on some bushes and none on others. Sometimes they are everywhere, sometimes nowhere. Skunks like to dig their dens in blueberry patches. Biting ants like to start their colonies near blueberry bushes.

These blueberries are easy to pick because they are growing on high, dry ground. Other species are found in swamps and bogs and may be scattered in their habitat. Still others may be in dry uplands, especially if the area had been ravaged by fires within the last several years.

One species often found growing among the blueberries is called the huckleberry. It grows in woods and thickets and clearings over a very wide area from Canada to Louisiana. Blueberry pickers often pick huckleberries, mix them in with the blueberries, and never know the difference.

Huckleberries are considered a separate genus, *Gaylussacia baccata*. They do not have a whitish bloom on their berries like blueberries. The berries are jet black and have ten seeds in them. Yet they are edible and taste enough like blueberries to be used with or as blueberries.

Blueberries are used for muffins and bread. Blueberry cream pie and blueberry ice cream are also favorites. They are among the more popular wild fruits for eating, and it takes relatively few to make up a good batch of wine.

Making Wild Blueberry Wine

Blueberry wine can be made with just one species of blueberry, or just huckleberry, or a mixture of species, depending on what is available. Each wine will be only slightly different, but it will be different.

If possible, gather only wild blueberries. Cultivated berries are usually not so sweet or flavorful. Wild ones are found somewhere or other in most eastern states and are ripe over a long season, from June to September. The same patch can produce continuously over a two month period.

Clean and wash three pints of blueberries. Mash them in a plastic pail, and add three pounds of sugar. Pour a gallon of boiling water on them and stir. When it reaches room temperature, add the wine yeast. Cover with cheesecloth. Let this work for ten days, stirring daily. Strain into a fermentation jug and water-seal. This will ferment for about six months. When it has quieted down, it can be bottled. This will be a very smooth wine—excellent for dinner.

HOPS

Most home winemakers have heard of at least one use for hops—every home beer drinker certainly has. What most of them do not know is that hops are wild herbaceous vines, which grow widely in the United States, Europe, and Asia. Hops are used to make beer, bitters, and ale. The common species of hop yards, *Humulus lupulus,* is grown commercially in Europe and the United States. Another species (*Humulus japonicus*) from East Asia has escaped from cultivation and grows wild from New England to Missouri.

Wild hops may be familiar to many people without their realizing it. I once saw a vine climbing up the side of a two-story house and asked the woman who lived there if she knew what it was. She didn't. The house was a hundred years old and the vine was probably older than she was. It was the common hops, producing abundant fruits.

My grandmother picked hops in the hop yards of Oregon many years ago, but she probably would not recognize it now. It would not occur to her that hops might be found growing wild a few hundred yards from her house, but they can be.

The name hops comes from the ancient Anglo-Saxon word "hop-pan" meaning "to climb." So look for hops in August hanging from trees and bushes along riverbanks.

Wild hops; *Humulus lupulus*

Wild hops grow in wetlands, rocky riverbanks, and in sandy places. An herbaceous, perennial vine, hops die back to the ground in the fall and sprout in the spring. It twines around trees, bushes, herbs, or anything else that is convenient and may grow ten meters long in the course of the summer.

Hop leaves are three-lobed. Their most distinguishing characteristic appears in August and September when the fruits ripen. They are yellow, cone-like bodies, each scale enclosing a seed within.

Hops have been used in food and medicine in addition to drink. The buds and tender young stems can be eaten in the spring, when they emerge from the ground. Pioneer women used hops in decoction with yeast to raise bread believing that the antiseptic qualities of the yeast would prevent bread from spoiling.

The fruiting hops contain lupulite, a bitter substance of value in brewing that is said to have medicinal value. Hop tea mixed with red pepper is supposed to help settle the stomach. Hops are also alleged to be a valuable sedative, curing insomnia, nervousness, and headaches. It is also supposed to cure gonorrhea, kill worms, and cure toothaches.

Making Wild Hop Wine

Hops, whether or not they cure anything, can also be used for wine. Pick three ounces of the fruits when they are reasonably ripe. When they have the yellow powder containing lupulite in them, a little goes a long way.

Put the hops, a half pound of raisins, and two and a half to three pounds (depending on the amount of alcohol desired) of sugar in a plastic pail. Add the juice of one lemon. Pour a gallon of boiling water over this and stir. When at room temperature, add the wine yeast. Cover with cheesecloth and let work for four to seven days, stirring daily. Then strain into a fermentation jug, and water-seal. Allow it to ferment to completion. Then transfer into an aging vessel. Since we have not tried this recipe, sample every three months to see if it is done.

This wine should not be the first one attempted by a beginning winemaker. It is said to be an unusual wine, not at all for everyone's taste.

ELDERBERRIES

Elderberries have long been held in high esteem for wine. The poisoning in the play *Arsenic and Old Lace* was carried out by dissolving arsenic in elderberry wine. This does not mean that elderberry wine goes best with arsenic, but it does go well with much else.

The elderberry has been called the English grape because of its popularity as wine in England. In the eighteenth century, laws were passed in Portugal requiring the destruction of all elder bushes in the port wine growing regions because large quantities of these were being added to the wine.

There are many beliefs associated with the elder. It is believed that Judas hanged himself on an elder tree and elder wood was used in the True Cross of Christ. (The same beliefs have also been attached to other trees.) Because of these beliefs, German peasants used to pray before an elder tree prior to cutting it down. The English believed that elder trees were immune to being struck by lightning.

Elderberry trees and bushes have one property that deserves respect—they are quite poisonous. Livestock have been poisoned by eating young growth of elder. Children have been poisoned when using the hollow stem for blowguns. The roots are the most poisonous part. The leaves can be ground up and the resulting juice sprayed on vegetable gardens to keep insects away.

The elderberry stems and twigs, though they can be poisonous, have been used for blowguns, shepherd's pipes, and even elk calls. In the spring, they are sometimes used to tap maple trees for syrup.

The berries, however, are edible. Elderberries are not very good when eaten raw because they are high in tannin and therefore very bitter. They are tasty, though, when prepared as elderberry jelly, combining equal parts elderberry juice and sumac extract. Elderberries are used in an assortment of other things, using the juice or dried berries.

There are about twenty species of elderberries found across Europe, Asia, and the United States, all of the genus *Sambucus*. Three species grow in the western United States, two in the east.

The most common elderberry growing in eastern United States is in fact called the common elderberry (*Sambucus canadensis*) and grows from Canada to Mexico. Though sometimes found growing

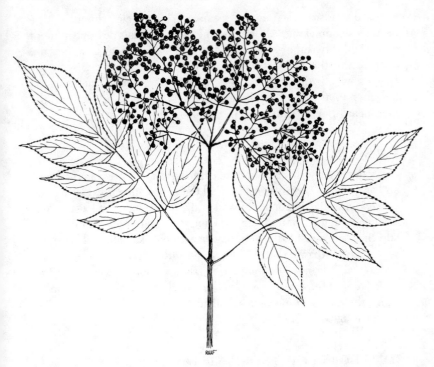

Common elderberry; *Sambucus canadensis*

along roadsides and railroad tracks, the common elderberry is most abundant in the moist, rich soil of river bottomlands. It is a small shrub, one to three meters tall, and has large compound leaves with about seven leaflets. Around June or July, large clusters of small white flowers are formed, which ripen into dark purple fruits in August and September. The tiny berries are not picked individually, but in clusters. Because of the long ripening season, you can harvest in a patch in late August and again about two weeks later.

Another common conspicuous, elderberry species has bright red fruits. It is the red-berried elder (*Sambucus pubens*) and is most common in woods and clearings across Canada and in northeastern United States. In early spring, it develops small clusters of cream-colored flowers, almost before the leaves are fully extended. In late June and July the fruits ripen into a bright red that is visible along forested roadsides at quite a distance. This species should not be used for winemaking. Although some plant manuals do not comment on its edibility, others state that the berry is poisonous. To be safe, avoid using the fruits of red-berried elderberries. Stick with the species with fruits that are dark when ripe, such as the common elderberry, the western species with blue-black berries, or the European species cultivated in this country.

Making Wild Elderberry Wine

Gather at least three pounds of elderberries. Remove all the bugs, and as much as possible, remove all the stems and twigs. Crush the berries in a plastic container and add three pounds of sugar. Pour a gallon of boiling water over it. When it cools to room temperature, add the wine yeast. Mix well. Cover with cheesecloth and let sit for seven days, stirring daily. Then strain into a fermentation jug and water-seal. Ferment to completion, then siphon into an aging jug.

Because of the high tannin levels, elderberry wine requires more aging than most. One and a half to two years should do it. The longer it ages, the better it gets.

HAWTHORNS OR THORNAPPLES

Hawthorns, also called thornapples, are members of the rose family and related to apples. Found throughout North America and Eurasia, they belong in the genus *Crataegus*.

The number of species of hawthorns that exist is unknown. In the United States alone, the number of species counted by botanists ranges from a hundred to a thousand. This is due to the great variability in the hawthorns and the great confusion they cause.

Hawthorns can vary in size from very low shrubs to small trees. They usually have two- to three-inch-long thorns. Their leaves, flowers, and fruits are different from tree to tree. Crossbreeding among species is common, which adds to the confusion. In order to identify an individual bush, a botanist collects a specimen when it is flowering and then again when it has ripe fruits, and is still sometimes wrong.

Typically, hawthorns are small trees, two or three meters tall, found in thickets, clearings, and old pastures. They can often be

recognized by their shape in old pastures where they space themselves out in orchard style. The long thorns of most species are
unmistakable. The leaves and small green fruits have some resemblance to apple.

The flowers appear in May or June. Each tree blooms only a short
period, but all the trees in the patch bloom at slightly different,
overlapping times.

The fruits are ripe in the fall after some hard frosts. They are

Hawthorn or thornapple; *Crataegus schuettei*

usually red or mostly red. Deer and birds feed on these. Squirrels like the thornapples, and mice will eat their seeds. Sometimes a tree will be stripped before it is ripe. Many insects and birds which would not otherwise visit the old pasture depend on hawthorns for food and shelter. They are among the more useful shrubs for wildlife.

Hawthorns have been cultivated in Europe for centuries as impenetrable hedges. The long, tough thorns are a powerful deterrent to trespassers.

The hawthorn was used in ancient Rome as a charm against sorcery and witchcraft. The Greeks used hawthorns to make marriage torches. Leaves were placed in the cradles of newborn babies to invoke a special blessing. Later, the hawthorn was believed to have special healing properties because it was supposedly used in Christ's crown of thorns.

The healing properties do in fact exist. A decoction of the ripe fruit acts to reduce hardening of the arteries. It helps heart valve defects, poor heart action, and hypertrophy. Studies have found that, in some patients, digitalis treatment could be reduced when hawthorn extract was administered.

Hawthorn fruits can be eaten raw, in jellies, and in marmalades. The best way to gather them is to find a patch, then go from tree to tree tasting them. Since many hawthorns are quite inedible raw, the occasional sweet ones should be remembered and returned to year after year. Remember, the more edible the raw fruit, the less aging time required for the finished wine.

Making Hawthorn or Thornapple Wine

Wash three quarts of fruit to remove dust. (This is especially important when picked near dirt roads.) Cut off the stems. Mash up the fruits in a plastic pail. Pour a gallon of boiling water over the fruit and add three pounds of sugar. When cool, add wine yeast and cover with cheesecloth. Stir daily for eight days. Strain into a fermentation jug and water-seal. After six weeks of fermenting, siphon into an aging jug. Bottle after about one year. Some wines may take longer to be ready, some less, depending on the quality of the fruit. Some may take longer to clear because of varying amounts of pectin.

Thornapple wine is an excellent wine, worth the trouble and the thorns to pick. It alone justifies the existence of those weedy trees along roadsides and pastures.

WILD STRAWBERRIES

Wild strawberries bear little resemblance to cultivated strawberries. Wild strawberries are barely a centimeter in diameter and often only a few to the plant. As they take a very long time to pick, most people do not bother. In terms of flavor, wild strawberries are more flavorful and sweeter than cultivated ones, which were bred for size.

The two species of strawberries found in eastern United States also are found all over the country. The differences between them are technical and not worth mentioning. Both produce good fruit.

The strawberry is a small plant of the rose family. Each leaf has three-toothed leaflets. The plant grows runners during the summer, from which new plants take root and grow. It produces white flowers in April and early May, then ripe fruits in June and early July.

Strawberries are not found everywhere in their range. Where they are found, they prefer sandy or well-drained locations. They also prefer sunny places and will produce more fruit in sunny places than in shady ones.

When hunting for wild strawberries to pick, look for a very large patch, where the berries are abundant. Many small roadside patches have barely a mouthful of berries on them.

The edible qualities and uses of wild strawberries are too numerous to mention and are the same as for the larger cultivated ones.

Making Wild Strawberry Wine

Strawberry wine is one in which some of the flavor of the berry comes through. Wash two quarts of wild strawberries, and remove the little green stems. Crush them in a plastic pail and add three pounds of sugar. Mix well. Pour a gallon of boiling water over this mixture. When cooled to room temperature, add wine yeast. Cover with cheesecloth and stir every day for ten days. Then strain into a fermentation jug and water-seal. Fermentation should take two months. Then siphon into an aging jug and allow to age for one

Wild strawberry; *Fragaria virginiana*

year. It will produce a dry wine that is good for casual drinking. If a sweet dessert strawberry wine is desired, increase the sugar to three and a half pounds.

Cactus

The cactus family is well known as a desert plant. The towering saguaro cactus is practically a symbol of the old cowboy movie. There are, however, many other kinds of cactus besides those seen in the movies.

The cactus family has at least 1,700 species, most of them growing in the desert of the Southwest and Mexico. Some are found in Central American rain forests, a few in parts of southern Canada, and a few more in suitable places in the eastern United States.

The eastern species of cactus are all part of the genus *Opuntia*, the prickly pears. One species or another is found in most states, in dry rocks, sand dunes, and sand prairies. They can be abundant in areas.

Two species, *Opuntia tortispina* and *Opuntia polyacantha*, are found in the western prairies and plains, occasionally reaching the Midwest.

Another species, the fragile prickly pear (*Opuntia fragilis*) is found across the west, east to Wisconsin and Illinois. It is a very small, prostrate cactus, whose fruit is inedible.

The common prickly pear of the east (*Opuntia compressa*), found in dry places from Massachusetts to southern Minnesota, south to Georgia and Missouri, can be recognized by its flat, usually spineless, jointed pads (leaves). It produces large yellow flowers in midsummer followed by edible red or purple fruits in fall.

Other species of prickly pear, mostly with spines, are found in the Southwest and Mexico. Mexican peasants eat half-grown prickly pear pads as a boiled vegetable, first removing the spines and skinning them. The California Indians cultivated prickly pears as fruit trees long before the discovery of America. Peeled stems were used to dress wounds as well.

Other species of prickly pear, mostly with spines, are found in Hawaii. The common one is *Opuntia megacantha*, locally called panini. Brought to Hawaii from Mexico in about 1809 by a Spaniard named Don Marin, it has become widespread. The reason for its

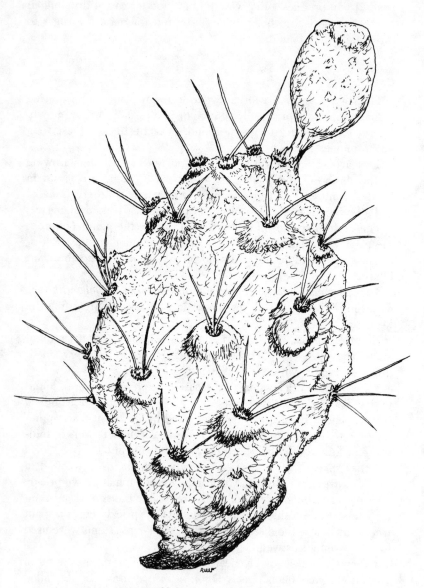

Prickly pear cactus; *Opuntia*

success in tropical islands lies in the climate and terrain. The trade winds all blow in one direction. On the windward side of the mountains, it can rain almost every day, as the breezes drop the moisture. On the leeward side, desert conditions exist. No desert plants existed there, so the prickly pear had no competition. The prickly pear is now found on dry Hawaiian mountainsides up to 2,000 feet.

When the prickly pear was introduced to Hawaii, its uses must also have been introduced. The ripe fruit is eaten fresh or fermented as a type of wine, as is done frequently in Mexico.

Making Cactus Wine

First, find a patch of prickly pear. Some areas have large patches. In the fall, gather five pounds or more of the red-purple fruit. Taste it to make sure it is ripe.

Slice the five pounds into a plastic pail and add three pounds of sugar. Pour a gallon of boiling water over this. Next day, add the wine yeast. Let work for about a week, then strain it into a fermentation jug, and water-seal. Ferment to completion, then siphon into an aging vessel and age for one year. Euell Gibbons would recommend adding a fifth of brandy to this wine to improve the flavor.

Chapter Four

Flower Wines

Most wild fruits are not ready to harvest until midsummer or fall. To keep busy prior to this time, the home winemaker can make wines from wildflowers.

Bouquets of wildflowers may be romantic to some people, but to a home winemaker, bouquets of wildflowers translate into bouquets of wine. The bouquet (scent or odor) of wildflower wines is their chief attraction. They will always be light, delicate wines with good bouquet, if the right amounts of each type of flower are used. Some flowers have more scent than others and will produce more bouquet per volume.

Wildflowers contain little sugar to contribute to the wine, and since they have no acid, it is often added. They have little or no tannin, but none is needed in this type of wine. Aging time is less in some cases, and flower wines clear easily.

Collect wildflowers on dry, sunny days after the dew has dried off of them. They will be fully open on these days and producing as much nectar as possible to attract flying insects. Wet flowers often have less scent than dry ones and what little scent remains may be lost in the collecting bag.

When collecting is completed, discard all green parts, including the flower sepals. Green parts add bitterness to many of these wines. Cowslip sepals and stems, for example, can and do add bitterness to cowslip wine. The milky sap of dandelion leaves, stems, and sepals is very bitter. The stems are not poisonous, only disagreeable.

While many flowers are safe to use in wines, not all flowers are. The rhododendron, common in the southern Appalachians, is quite poisonous. Honey made from rhododendron flowers is extremely toxic and must be discarded. The reason for the toxicity of the rhododendron is a drug found in the pollen. Other flowers may have other drugs in them that make them more or less toxic. Lilac flowers, for instance, are extremely toxic, but some adventurous winemakers make and drink lilac wine. We less adventurous types, however, tend to avoid plants that someone else regards poisonous. They probably found out the hard way.

The flower wines described in this chapter have all been made into wine and are known to be safe. Other wildflowers not listed here can be safely made into wine if you want to experiment. Make quite certain first that they are safe. Consult books on edible plants and poisonous plants before starting out. There may be some great new wines out there to explore.

One possible example is the day lily (*Hemerocallis fulva*). Found as a wild roadside weed in much of the country, it forms beds of many basal leaves. Its flowering stalks come up in July to bloom only one day. The tubers, young shoots, buds, flowers, and spent flowers are all edible. The flower tastes somewhat like green beans when cooked. Yet I could not find a day lily wine recipe. It could be a winner.

Some flower wine recipes call for hot water, but some recommend cold water to cut down on destruction of the natural perfumes. This is a matter of personal preference. Some recipes call for addition of lemon juice to add acid. All require following the recommended quantities of flowers, to give the wines their proper strength. When measuring flowers, pack the container lightly, just enough to settle the flowers, not mash them.

If you would prefer light, sweet dessert wines, then wildflower wines are for you. They are fun to pick, easy to prepare, and entirely drinkable.

FLOWERING SHRUBS

Many wines can be made from the delicately scented flowers of shrubs that bloom in early summer. Some of these shrubs have been discussed previously for their excellent fruit wines.

Hawthorn (or Thornapple) Wine

Hawthorns can be used for wine long before the hard frosts by making hawthorn flower wine. Go to the hawthorn patch in late May or early June when it is in full bloom. Walk from tree to tree smelling the blossoms. Pick a half gallon of the flowers that produce the strongest fragrance, being careful not to get stung by bees.

Put the flowers in the bottom of a plastic pail. Pour a gallon of water (hot or cold) over them. Add the juices of one lemon and one orange and three and a half pounds of sugar. When the mixture is at room temperature, add the wine yeast. Stir thoroughly. Cover with cheesecloth and let stand for two weeks, stirring daily. Strain into a fermentation vessel and water-seal. Allow to ferment to completion, then sample. If aging is required, siphon to an aging vessel and let stand for up to one year.

Hawthorn flowers are prized for their wines, more so than the fruits. This will make an excellent sweet wine.

Rose Wine

The fruits are not the only part of wild roses that are edible and medicinal, the flowers are as well. Distilled rose petal water has been used since ancient times. It has been used to treat eye irritations. The Aztecs used it as a purgative. The ancient Romans mixed it into their food and wines, and the wealthy sometimes filled their fountains with it. Once used for baptisms, it is a favorite cosmetic for Eurasian women and forms the basis of American cosmetics and hand lotions.

Rose petals are used in many dishes by inventive cooks, such as rose syrup, rose petal jam, candied rose petals, and rose petal pancakes. Roses, beautiful as they are to look at, are delicious to eat.

Pick wild roses in June or July when they bloom. The more scented they are, the less that are needed. Some recipes call for a pint of flowers per gallon of water, others for a half gallon of flowers per gallon of water. A larger amount of roses will produce a much stronger bouquet.

However many roses you use, clean them and put them in a plastic pail. Pour a gallon of boiling water over them. Add three pounds of sugar and the juice of two lemons. When it cools to room temperature, add the wine yeast. Stir, cover with cheesecloth, and let stand for six days, stirring daily. Then strain into a fermentation jug and water-seal. Allow this to ferment to completion. Sample, and if necessary, age up to a year.

Elder Blossom Wine

One of the best known flower wines is made from the flowers of the elderberry. This is particularly true in Britain. Elderflower wine is not appreciated by everyone who tries it. It is an acquired taste. If it is too strong it can be horrible.

Various recipes call for various amounts of flowers. Some call for a pint of flowers per gallon of water, some say that is too much. One calls for a *gallon* of flowers per gallon of water. This is probably way too much.

Pick between a pint and a quart of elderflowers. The common elder flowers in July and is visible at some distance. You can shake the flowers off the branches or break off the whole flower cluster from the bush.

Separate the flowers from the stalks and wash off the insects. Put the elderflowers in a plastic pail. Add the juice and grated rinds of one lemon and one orange. Pour a gallon of boiling water over this. Add three pounds of sugar. Stir. When cooled to room temperature, add the wine yeast. Cover the pail and let sit for six days, stirring daily. Strain into a fermentation jug and water-seal. Let work until completion. Sample, and if necessary, age up to six months.

For a sweeter wine, add another half pound of sugar.

Leftover flowers can be fried in batter or put in pancakes or muffins. Never waste a wild food.

Meadowsweet (Spiraea) Wine

Meadowsweets are small shrubs of the rose family in the genus *Spiraea*. Five native species are described in the northeastern United States, some widely ranging. Two of the species are of limited range in the southern Appalachians. The other three are widely ranging across eastern Canada, south to Missouri and North Carolina. They are closely related to the Japanese lilac or Japanese spiraea of backyards and gardens.

From June to August, all native species of meadowsweet form dense clusters of small, five-petaled flowers. In some species, such as the white meadowsweet (*Spiraea alba*) the flowers are always white. In most others, like the hardhack (*Spiraea tomentosa*) the flowers are pink to purple.

Look for meadowsweets in wet meadows, swamps, and along riverbanks. They prefer sunny areas. If you have seen Japanese lilacs, you will readily recognize the wild species. Where they are found, meadowsweets form large patches of shrubs, very often one to two meters tall. Numerous clusters of flowers are formed on each bush in June and July. While there may still be some straggling blooms in August, they are well past their peak.

Other parts of meadowsweets are collected for their medicinal value. Leaves and stems have been decocted for use as a cure for stomach disorders. Boiled stems are used for tea, and boiled roots have been used for diarrhea.

Because the flowers have a delicate flavor, pick a gallon of them, removing from the stems. White or purple flowers can be used, depending on which species is available. (Japanese lilac could also be used.)

Wash the flowers and place them in a plastic pail. Add three and a half pounds of sugar and the juices of two lemons. Pour a gallon of boiling water over this. When it cools to room temperature, add the wine yeast. Cover and let sit for five or six days, stirring daily. Strain into a fermentation jug and water-seal. Ferment to completion. Sample, and age as needed, perhaps six months. It will produce a delicate, sweet dessert wine.

Honeysuckle Wine

Wild honeysuckles are bushes or vines of various sizes. They are

Tartarian honeysuckle; *Lonicera tatarica*

87

most easily recognized by their five-lobed, usually yellow, tubular
flowers.

A dozen species are found in the northeastern United States.
Some are several meters tall, others are very short, such as the
Mountain Fly-Honeysuckle (*Lonicera villosa*) found in bogs in
Canada and the northern-most United States. This one has few
flowers anyway and is unlikely to be picked for wine.

Other larger species have an abundance of flowers. The Wild
Honeysuckle (*Lonicera dioica*) is a climbing shrub covered with red
and yellow flowers. It is found growing in wet woods, thickets, and
sometimes rocky places across Canada and south to Oklahoma.

Another, perhaps more accessible honeysuckle is the *Tartarian*
Honeysuckle (*Lonicera tatarica*). It is frequently cultivated, but is
very often found growing wild in waste places and thickets. It is
what is called the "bird-berry bush," for the attractive red and
orange double berries formed in June and July. In spring, it
produces an abundance of light pink flowers that cover the bush for
a short season. Gather the flowers quickly, while the bush is in full
bloom.

Look for the blooms of honeysuckle anytime between April and
June. They are easy to recognize in the thickets, wetlands, and
waste places where they grow. Many species are quite widespread,
and some grow near just about everybody.

The flowers of any of the dozen species can be used for wine. Pick
a half gallon of the flowers, and put them in a plastic pail. To make
a dry wine, add two and a half pounds of sugar. To make a sweet
wine, add three and a half pounds. Pour a gallon of boiling water
over this and stir. Add the juices of two lemons. When cool, add
a campden tablet to kill off any undesirable microbes. The next day,
add the wine yeast. Cover with cheesecloth and let it work for three
or four days, stirring daily. Strain into a fermentation jug and water-
seal. Ferment to completion. Sample when complete, but age for
six months before bottling.

DANDELION

The common dandelion is one plant that is never far from most
winemakers. It grows almost everywhere and especially favors areas
disturbed by man. Many a green lawn may be covered by dande-

Meadowsweet; *Spiraea alba*

lions. The more effort made to get rid of them, the better they grow.

Many people like dandelions and see the cheery yellow blooms as a convincing sign of spring. They aren't bothered by the presence of dandelions, and sometimes they make good use of them. The early spring leaves of the dandelion can be eaten as a vegetable. Dandelions, like lettuce, must be harvested before the bitter milky sap develops in the leaves. The leaves can also be used as seasoning and in salads.

The roots of dandelion can be roasted and ground up for a caffeine-free coffee. They are sometimes used for home root beers, too.

Dandelion flowers can be picked any time from March to November. Their peak blooming season and the best time to pick them by far is in April or May, when dandelion patches are covered with flowers.

For all practical purposes, there is is only one species of dandelion to consider. It is highly variable plant, growing long stems in fields and short stems in lawns where they have to duck under lawnmowers. European botanists have studied dandelions for centuries. By studying variations of the flower ovaries, striations of the achenes, and assorted other microscopic differences, they have described and named 5,000 different species. Most of these are probably not species, just genetic variations within the specimens used to make the study. For the average dandelion picker, a dandelion is a dandelion.

Making Dandelion Wine

A lot of dandelions are required for this wine recipe. Pick six quarts of flowers and remove the flower heads. The green sepals and the stems, if added, will make a harsh wine. Since dandelions are so abundant, get enough for six quarts without the stems, sepals, and heads.

Put four quarts of the dandelion flowers in a plastic container. Thinly slice two lemons and two oranges into the flowers. Pour in one gallon of boiling water. Let stand for ten days, stirring daily. Keep this mixture well covered to prevent contamination with wild yeast. After ten days strain off the liquid and squeeze all remaining liquid out of the pulp. Bring the liquid to a boil and add three pounds of sugar, cutting off the heat as soon as the sugar dissolves.

Pour back into the plastic container and add a pound of raisins.

Allow to cool to room temperature and add the wine yeast. As soon as a vigorous fermentation is in progress (lots of bubbling), add the remaining two quarts of dandelion flowers. This is done to add what bouquet was lost during the boiling process. Allow to ferment on this pulp for seven to ten days, stirring daily.

Strain off the liquid into fermentation jugs with a water-seal. Do not fill the jug all the way to the top but leave a little space in the neck. Let the wine ferment for two weeks. Then feed it every four or five days with small amounts of sugar. (The feeding technique is often used in winemaking to increase the alcohol content.) When the jug is too full to continue feeding, simply let the wine ferment to completion.

Siphon the wine into an aging jug and allow to age for six months. If the wine has cleared, siphon into wine bottles. If the wine has not cleared, suspend bentonite wrapped in cheesecloth in a funnel. Bentonite, a clay used for clearing wine, can be purchased in hobby shops. Siphon the wine through it. The wine should clear in a week. After bottling, age for six more months.

This produces a sweet, full-bodied, white dessert wine. It is a distinctly flavored wine, which is somewhat acid at first. The acidity will decline with aging.

Many dandelion wine recipes exist. Whichever one you use, be sure to age the wine as directed. The longer it ages, the better the wine. I heard of a home wine drinker who inherited a small quantity of twenty-year-old dandelion wine. It was outstanding—the acidity was gone.

VIOLETS

Violets, in my opinion, are the most beautiful wildflowers. Their delicate blue blossoms with black streaks on the bottom petal are a sure sign that spring has arrived.

There are many species of violets. They are all low plants, mostly with round green leaves. Some are stemless, sprouting leaves from a ground-hugging rhizome. Others are stemmed and, in at least one yellow-flowered species, may grow to a half meter tall.

Fifty species may be found in the northeastern United States. Some are found in bogs and in swamps. Some are found only in cool, rocky woods, and others make their homes only on sand plains.

A few are wide ranging, growing in forests, fields, and lawns. One
species turns up abundantly just before Mother's Day each year.

The flowers of violets vary greatly from species to species. The
widely ranging Bird's Foot Violet (*Viola pedata*) whose leaves are
shaped like bird's feet, has flowers that may be several centimeters
across. Pansies that have escaped from flower beds are also violets.

Some species have white flowers, such as the Wild White Violet

(*Left*) blue marsh violet; *Viola cucullata*, (*right*) stemmed white violet; *Viola
canadensis*

(*Viola pallens*). The flowers tend to be very small. This species is found mostly in cool, wet places in the north.

Other violets have yellow flowers. Two widely ranging species, *Viola eriocarpa* and *Viola pubescens,* are very common in some places.

One species is purple on the underside of the petals, white on the upperside, and yellow down inside the flower. This is the Canada violet (*Viola canadensis*) found in rich woods.

All the various species of violets have one thing in common: they are all spring flowering plants, blooming sometime between April and June. A few of them will produce in September and October as well. However, spring is violet-picking time.

The violet has long been held in high esteem by man. It was the national flower of Athens back when Athens was the cradle of democracy. The Romans drank a perfumed wine made from violets. Poultices of violet were used to cure skin cancer as long ago as 500 B.C. When Napoleon was exiled to Elba, his partisans used the violet as a secret recognition badge. Violet tea was a favorite drink of European aristocrats at one time.

Violets still capture the imagination today. The "wood violet" is the state wildflower of Wisconsin. The legislature has even debated just which species of violet this is intended to be.

Violets have made their way into folk songs. "Violets of Dawn" was recorded by Eric Anderson some years back, and more recently violets are mentioned in "Houses" written and recorded by Judy Collins.

Violets have been used for medicinal purposes. A syrup of violets and honey has been used as a children's laxative. Violets were used as a sedative in Greek times and to cure a wide variety of ills throughout the Middle Ages.

Whether or not they work on most ailments is debatable, but violets will cure vitamin deficiency. The flowers and leaves contain more vitamin C than any garden vegetable. The leaves also are rich in vitamin A.

The leaves are picked and eaten in salads or cooked as greens. The flowers are used to make jam, jelly, syrup, candy, and wine.

When picking the flowers for any of these uses, do not worry about damaging the violet population, as long as the plants aren't pulled out by the roots. Most violets are perennial, coming up year after year. They produce few seeds from their beautiful flowers, so it doesn't hurt seed production to pick them. Most violet seeds are produced during the summer, in small flowers that are borne near the ground but never open. They self-pollinate and split open when the seeds are mature.

Still, it is best to pick only the more common types of violets in an area. And if it is a well-travelled area, leave some for other people to look at and enjoy.

Some violet species are scented, some are not. Flowers for wine are best if they are scented. Another consideration is size. The larger the flower, the fewer need to be picked.

It does not take long to pick enough violets for wine. I took a winemaking friend to a moist riverbottom forest to pick violets one May. We were picking the wooly blue violet (*Viola sororia*), a large, deep-blue species. I had picked violets before for jelly and only needed two cups. I wasn't sure how many were needed for wine, but he insisted it was two quarts.

So we picked and picked. Since the violets are so close to the ground, it was back-breaking work. The first hatch of mosquitoes that May attacked us at every opportunity.

Finally, when we had strained our backs, he decided that the three quarts we had picked looked like two quarts. So we took them home and he never looked at the recipe until the violets were in the pail. Even though the recipe called for two cups, he used three quarts. He was going to get a bouquet out of his wine if it knocked him unconscious.

Making Violet Wine

The recipe should be varied to suit the species of violet used. A scented one requires fewer violets than an unscented one.

For starters, pick two cups of violets or pansies. If the first batch of wine isn't strong enough, use more the next time.

Put the fresh blossoms in a plastic pail. Pour a gallon of boiling water over them. Mix in three pounds of sugar. Add the rinds of two lemons and one orange, and the juices of one orange and one lemon. When the mixture has cooled to room temperature, add the wine yeast and cover with cheesecloth. Stir daily for ten days, then strain into a fermentation jug and water-seal. When fermentation has ceased, bottle. Age for about one year.

This will be a sweet after-dinner wine, which has been consumed after many a dinner since Roman times.

COWSLIPS

While most marsh plants do not start to bloom until the middle of the summer, the cowslip is a very early spring bloomer. It appears before most other plants have started to leaf out.

The cowslip (*Caltha palustris*) is a small herb of marshes, streambanks, and other wetlands found across northern North America and northern Europe, and Asia. In the United States, it is found south to Indiana and Iowa.

The cowslip has heart-shaped, dark green leaves that appear with the flowers in the spring. The flowers are bright yellow and several centimeters across. Since they bloom before the marsh vegetation is grown, they are visible at quite a distance.

Though all cowslips look much alike and are considered one species, genetic studies have suggested a number of separate, geographically distinct breeding populations of cowslips.

The cowslip, also called marsh marigold, is a member of the buttercup family. There are many more common names, mostly in England. Common names of well-known plants vary from locality to locality, but in America a cowslip is a cowslip.

As a medicine, the cowslip is used to treat warts. It has been used for cough syrups and in treating anemia.

Cowslip leaves can be eaten as greens. They contain a poison, however, that must be boiled out. They are nutritious, being full of vitamins C and A.

Cowslip buds can be pickled, made into a sauce, or candied. They also should have the poison boiled out, since the stems contain a small amount of it.

Apparently the only use of the opened flowers is for wine. Gather them on a dry, sunny, spring day. They can be found by driving along country roads, watching every wet spot. The blooming season is relatively short, in April or early May, but when they bloom, the whole patch blooms.

It is usually necessary to wear boots when picking cowslips, often

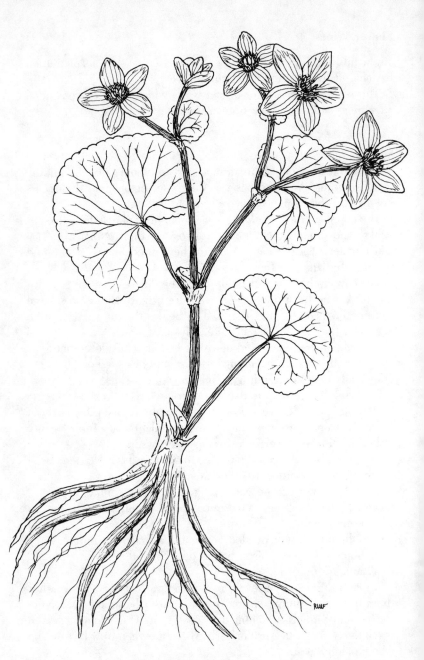

Cowslip or marsh marigold; *Caltha palustris*

hip boots. If it is a warm day and not quite mosquito season, old tennis shoes and shorts will do, though the water will be cold.

Make sure the flowers are dry. Wet flowers will wilt or discolor in the collecting bag. Pick only fresh yellow blooms, not old faded ones that have started to turn white. Quality blossoms always make a quality wine.

Making Cowslip Wine

Gather at least two quarts of the blossoms. That much is needed because not all the flavor is extracted from the blossoms.

To prepare the flowers, remove the stems. They contain a bit of the bitter poison and are not wanted. When all the flowers have been cleaned, place them in a plastic pail.

Pour a gallon of boiling water over them. Add three pounds of white sugar, the juice of half a lemon, and one half pound of raisins. When cooled to room temperature, add the wine yeast. Once fermentation has started, stir this everyday for two weeks. Then strain into a fermentation jug. Allow to ferment to completion. Feeding with small amounts of sugar from time to time will increase the alcohol content.

When the fermentation is complete, the wine will clear inside of two or three days. Siphon it into an aging vessel and allow to age for six to eight months. Then bottle and age another six months.

Other recipes call for using brown sugar or adding hops, brandy, or briar twigs.

The recipes in British winemaking books and in American books derived from British sources were not written with this species in mind. They are referring to *Primula veris*, a member of the primrose family that is common in England, which is always called cowslip there. Our cowslip (*Caltha*) is also common in England, but has different common names. However, the cowslip recipes in those books can be used for our cowslips.

A friend who makes a lot of cowslip wine recommends the following recipe:

Pour the water over the blossoms and let stand for ten days. Then without straining, bring the must to a boil and simmer for three minutes. Cool, add three pounds sugar, yeast, and one half pound of raisins. Ferment for seven days, stirring daily. Then strain, put into fermentation vessels, and ferment to completion. Siphon into an aging vessel and age for six months. Bottle and age another six months.

The must, when boiled, is liable to give off a very unpleasant odor, much like the odor given off by wet boots when you come out of your favorite cowslip marsh, but fear not. I almost discarded my entire stock of cowslip wine must when this strange aroma assailed my nostrils, but luckily I took a chance. One year later I was rewarded with some of the finest, delicate white wine that I have ever tasted.

FLOWERS OF THE MEADOW

Having covered flowering shrubs and a few flowers of forest, marsh, and lawn, we now come to an assortment of flowers commonly found growing in meadows and waste places. They all bloom during the summer and are all often abundant where they do grow.

Daisy

The common ox-eye daisy (*Chrysanthemum leucanthemum*), abundant throughout much of the United States, is a migrant from Europe. It has small, irregularly-lobed leaves and numerous flowers, which are yellow in the center with white petals or rays.

The daisy is a perennial, coming up year after year. Flowers usually appear in June, but can be found into October. In June, a meadow or waste field might have thousands of blooming daisies per acre.

Picking daisies can be a pleasant task. The terrain is generally high and dry. The meadows are open, and mosquitoes usually do not venture out into the June sunshine, preferring swamps and woods by day. The weather is much better than spring flower season.

Pour a gallon of water (hot or cold) over a gallon of clean, fresh daisies. Let this stand for two days. Then strain off the liquid, squeezing the blossoms to get all the flavor and juice. Dissolve three pounds of sugar in the liquid and add the wine yeast. Cover the pail with cheesecloth and let it ferment for two weeks, stirring daily. Transfer to a fermentation jug and water-seal. Ferment to completion and allow to clear. Siphon into wine bottles. No aging is necessary for this wine.

Chamomile

A somewhat similar plant is the chamomile (*Anthemis nobilis*) which has daisy-like flowers but more finely divided leaves. Native

Ox eye daisy; *Chrysanthemum leucanthemum*

to Europe, it is grown as an herb and is escaped here and there in the United States. They bloom from July on.

Chamomile is a medicinal herb. One ounce to one pint of boiling water can be used to stimulate stomach action. The flower is used as a poultice to relieve pain. A lotion of chamomile is used to relieve earaches and toothaches.

Recipes can be found for chamomile tea and beer, and chamomile syrup is a popular medicinal recipe.

This particular wine is said to be excellent, provided the wine-maker does not go overboard on the amount of flowers. Chamomile flowers have a powerful fragrance, which can be overpowering.

Put one pint to one quart of the flowers in a plastic pail. Pour a gallon of boiling water over them. Add three and a half pounds of sugar and the juice of two lemons. When cool, add the wine yeast and let it work for five days, stirring daily. Then strain into a fermentation jug, water-seal. Let it ferment completely. Age as needed.

A similar-looking herb, far more common than chamomile in the United States, is wild chamomile (*Matricaria chamomilla*), also called German chamomile. It is also used as an herb and in tea. It can also be used for wine and would make a slightly different flavored wine. Also from Europe, it is found in waste areas and roadsides and is the one you will most likely find.

Red Clover

The red clover (*Trifolium pratense*) is a very common plant of roadsides, meadows, and pastures. It is frequently cultivated, for as a legume it enriches the soil with nitrogen as well as being a good component of hay.

Red clover blooms all summer, but it is most abundantly flowered in June. Its red-flowering heads are actually clusters of numerous small flowers.

Red clover is another plant that has medicinal uses. Red clover tea made from dried leaves has been used to "cleanse the blood" in the spring and provide needed nutrients. It has been used for hoarseness and ulcers, and is said to have sedative qualities. Bathing sores on the skin with a red clover infusion helps to clear them up.

Red clover can also be mildly poisonous. There are cases of hay

Wild chamomile or German chamomile; *Matricaria chamomilla*

containing large quantities of late season red clover causing a slobbering syndrome in cattle, horses, and sheep. However, in order for the symptoms to occur at least ten pounds per day had to be ingested for three days straight.

Do not worry about clover wine being poisonous. Only the flower heads are used, and the extract is quite dilute. In any case, very large quantities would have to be drunk.

Get three quarts of lightly packed heads and place them in a plastic pail. Add a gallon of boiling water, three and a half pounds of sugar, and the juice of one lemon. When cool, add yeast and let work for five days, stirring daily. Then strain into a fermentation jug and ferment to completion. Little or no aging is required.

A very similar recipe calls for four quarts of flowers, the juices of two oranges and three lemons and four pounds of sugar. This wine would be more acid, but sweeter. A month of aging is recommended.

Other clovers might also be used for wine. One of them, *Alsike* clover (*Trifolium hybridum*), is a natural crossbreed between red clover and white clover. It is long-stemmed like red clover, but has white-flowered heads with pink around the base. This one is not as scented as red clover, so would probably make a lower quality wine.

The other likely wine candidate is the white clover (*Trifolium repens*). It is common in lawns and fields and blooms greatly in early summer.

Vervain

The vervains, or verbenas, are a group of small herbs with (usually) purple or lavender flowers. There are half a dozen species found in the northeastern United States that all look fairly similar. They can be found in sandy waste areas, roadsides, prairies, fields, and sometimes moist places. Their spikes of flowers usually only have a few flowers open at a time, and it can take a long time to gather them. They bloom from June until August.

Vervain has a rich past for so nondescript an herb. It was used as a tonic and expectorant. It was valuable for treating nerves, scurvy, and worms. In the Middle Ages, it was used for witchcraft protection. It was used as a pledge of mutual good faith. For a time

Blue vervain; *Verbena hastata*

people believed if the dining room was sprinkled with vervain tea before a party, the guests would be merrier.

About a quart of flowers are needed. Put them in a plastic pail. Boil three pounds of sugar in a gallon of water until dissolved. Then allow to cool a little and pour on the flowers. When at room temperature, add the wine yeast. Let work for a week, stirring daily. Strain into a fermentation jug and ferment to completion. Transfer to an aging vessel and age for four to six months.

Goldenrod

Every August, when the goldenrods cover the fields and roadsides with their yellow flowers, the hay fever sufferers start to complain. But goldenrod cannot be the cause of their hay fever, because its pollen does not blow through the air. The bright yellow flowers and sweet nectar attract insects, which carry the pollen. The real culprit of hay fever is the ragweed, whose flowers are green, unscented, and inconspicuous. They scatter their pollen to the wind and do not need to attract insects.

There are about fifty species of goldenrod in the northeastern United States. They are generally rather difficult to tell apart. All bloom in August and September. Most are roadside and field herbs, less than a meter tall.

One species is distinctive for its scented foliage Sweet goldenrod (*Solidago odora*) has anise-scented leaves. It is found from Massachusetts to southern Missouri and southward. This is the species Euell Gibbons referred to when he told us that goldenrod makes an excellent tea.

Another species that can be readily recognized is the bog goldenrod (*Solidago uliginosa*). It is about the only goldenrod adapted to bogs and swamps.

A third one and very common one, is canadian goldenrod (*Solidago canadensis*). It has very large flower clusters. The plants grow in dense groups from the same root system. It can be readily identified with practice.

Goldenrod has been of little use to man. Indians used powdered goldenrod leaves on sores on their horses. They also extracted a yellow dye from the flowers.

Goldenrods have sometimes been toxic to horses and sheep when

Common goldenrod or Canadian goldenrod; *Solidago canadensis*

ingested in large quantities. This has been attributed to the gold-enrod being infected with a fungal disease that produced a toxin.

Wine can be safely made from the flowers of any or all species of goldenrod. One recipe calls for a gallon of flowers, another only a pint. The amount needed varies with the species and the amount of scent it gives off.

Pour a gallon of warm water over a pint of flowers in a plastic pail and add three pounds sugar. Stir well and add the juices of six oranges. When at room temperature, add the wine yeast. Cover and let stand five days, stirring daily. Strain into a fermentation vessel and ferment to completion. Age if needed, but no more than six months.

Honey Wines

Though honey wines are not made directly from flowers, they are produced from flowers by bees. Different flowers produce different honeys, and therefore different wines.

There are three ways to get honey. One is to buy it from the supermarket, where its flower source may be unknown. Another is to buy it from a beekeeper, whose hives are in a known place with known flowers nearby. Though the bees will visit a variety of flowers, if one is particularly common, that will be the main source of the honey. The third way to get honey is to steal it from wild honeybees. This requires protective clothing and netting and is not recommended for people allergic to bee stings.

Wild bee nests are often found in hollow trees, but may be in old buildings. The best way to find them, other than by accident, is to locate a flower patch with large numbers of honeybees. If they are all from one nest, they will all go in the same direction when they have a full load. Their nest is probably within a mile of the patch. Bees will tend to make a beeline to their nest, so follow them. Once the nest is located, it will take bravery and fortitude to get the wild honey, but it can be done.

Some flowers produce better honey than others. Rhododendron and azalea produce poisonous honey. Basswood and linden produce excellent honey. When basswood and lindens bloom, they are constantly visited by a wide variety of insects by day and another wide variety at night. Honeybees love these two trees.

Clover also makes good honey. With its abundant nectar and fragrance, red clover would make a delicious honey, I'm sure, if only the honeybees could extract the honey. Honeybees can, however, readily pollinate and extract nectar from white clovers. In fact, a hive near a large white clover field is sure to produce excellent quality honey.

Honey, of course, has many uses. It is used as a spread on toast or for jam or jelly and is sometimes used as a sugar substitute.

Honey also is sometimes used in wine recipes, replacing part or all of the sugar required. It is also used as a wine by itself. There are a variety of recipes for honey wine, called mead in "merrie olde Englande."

If you have gathered honey from the wild, remove it from the honeycombs and strain it. Mix four pounds of honey with a gallon of water, the juice and thin-sliced rind of a lemon, and (optionally) two sticks of cinnamon. Boil this mixture for half an hour, then pour into a plastic pail and allow to cool. Add the wine yeast. Let stand several days, stirring daily. Then strain into a fermentation jug and water-seal. Ferment to completion and allow to clear. Bottle, or drink. Mead requires little aging and does not improve much thereafter.

Chapter Five

Shoot Wines

Shoot wines are those made from above-ground parts of the plant other than flowers and fruits. The portion of a plant that is above ground is called the shoot, the part below ground is (usually) the root. Wine ingredients that must be dug out of the ground are discussed in chapter six.

Wines made from plant shoots will have a different character than those made from fruits and flowers. They lack the sugars and aromas that flower and fruit wines have. Not all will be readily (or ever) appreciated by some winedrinkers, still some of them are highly recommended.

In the case of herbaceous plants (those that aren't woody) the leaves and stems are used. Usually only the leaves of woody plants are used, though in some cases the sap is also used to make a viable wine. The flowers, fruits, and roots of most of these plants cannot be used for wines.

A wide assortment of plants are included here, from forest trees to an assortment of common weeds. A large assortment of flavoring and seasoning herbs are also included.

Since these shoot wines are a motley assortment, and not all favored by most wine drinkers, wait to try them until you have attempted a few flower or fruit wines. As you gain experience, if something sounds worth a try and is readily available, try it. If it tastes terrible, you will know the main ingredient is at fault, not your winemaking skills.

TREE SAP WINES

During late summer and early fall, trees move sugars down to their roots to store for the winter. If they are spring flowering trees, they also develop the flower buds on their twigs. Later they lose their leaves and wait for spring.

In late winter, as soon as there are thawing days on a regular basis, trees begin transporting these sugars back up the trunk to start the development of flower and leaf buds. All trees do this, but the sap production is variable. Some use little sap in producing buds. Euell Gibbons tapped a basswood tree from January until it fully leafed out and never saw a drop of sap. Other trees have a lot of sap with little sugar in it. Still others have a very short sap season. Only two types of trees are regularly tapped for their saps, the maples and birches.

Maples

The common maple of upland forests is familiar to all. The pointed, lobed leaves are well-known shapes to leaf rakers. The winged seeds, produced during the summer, are a key characteristic of all maples.

Maples are known for their sap, which is converted to syrup and sugar. The amount of sap required to produce a gallon of syrup or a pound of sugar varies from species to species.

The maple with the most sugar is the sugar maple (*Acer saccharum*). It is found from New Brunswick to Tennessee to Minnesota. Its leaves tend to be five-lobed. It is very common in rich upland woods where it sometimes reaches a height of 40 meters.

Sugar maple syrup making is a major industry in New England and parts of the upper midwest. From 2 to 6 percent of sugar maple sap is sugar, and about thirty gallons of sap are needed to make a gallon of syrup or four pounds of sugar.

Maple syrup season runs from one to six weeks, depending on the weather, and occurs anytime between February and April. From five to forty gallons may be drawn from each tree, depending on size and location.

To collect maple sap, buy a metal spile (spout). During sap season, drill a hole about five centimeters deep into the sunny side of a sugar maple tree. (The trunk of the tree should be at least thirty-one centimeters or one foot in diameter.) Tap the spile in, and hang

Sugar maple; *Acer saccharum*

a gallon bucket on it. Several taps can be made on one tree, but only a gallon of sap is required for maple wine.

Other ways to get maple sap include buying it from a commercial sugarbush or from an amateur maple syrup maker.

The gathering of sugar maple sap and making of maple sugar was taught to us by the Indians. It was first described about 1700. Maple sugar was the only sugar the Ojibwa Indians had, and they made the most of it. At maple sugar time, each family moved to its own sugarbush area. It had a maple-sugar-making lodge and a storage lodge there. The average family tapped about 900 trees. Before kettles were introduced, they boiled down the sap by throwing hot stones into bark or wood vessels. Alternatively, they let the sap freeze, skimming out the ice.

The Indians used maple sugar in many foods, much as we use cane and beet sugar today. They used it as a syrup to get children to swallow medicine, and dissolved it in water for a summer drink. But they apparently never used it in wine.

Maple sap wine is an above-average shoot wine. It contains some sugars and tannins, but no strong constituents. It clears very easily.

Put one gallon of sugar maple sap and two and a half pounds of sugar in a pan and bring it to a boil. Boil for about fifteen minutes. In a separate pan, put the thinly peeled rind of one lemon, one-half cup of sap, and one-half ounce of cloves. Bring this to a boil and simmer for ten minutes. Mix all this in a plastic container with the juice of one lemon. Add wine yeast when cool. Stir daily for eight days, then strain into a fermentation jug and water-seal. Fermentation will cease in about six weeks. When done, siphon into an aging vessel and age one year.

This recipe can be made using a gallon of sap from other maples. Most are less sugary, so a bit more sugar may have to be added.

The black sugar maple (*Acer nigrum*) is very similar to the sugar maple and is said to be just as sugary. Its leaves tend to be three-lobed, however. Its range is similar to that of sugar maple, but it is most common in the western parts of its range. It is often tapped for its sugar.

Another common maple, the silver maple (*Acer saccharinum*), also has a range similar to that of the sugar maple, but a bit farther south. Sharper indentations on its leaves and bright red spring flowers are sure identifying marks. This tree is often cultivated in cities, but prefers river bottomlands. A fine sugar can be made from it, but the yield per tree is low.

A wide-ranging species is the red maple (*Acer rubrum*). Found from Canada to Texas, it prefers swamps, sometimes reaching a large size there. This tree also produces a sap, but it is less sweet than sugar maple and the yield is lower.

Two small maples, striped maple (*Acer pennsylvanicum*) and mountain maple (*Acer spicatum*), are of no use for sap. They reach the size of small trees in the Great Smoky Mountains but are merely shrubs elsewhere.

The box elder (*Acer negundo*) is a maple that doesn't look like a maple. It has compound leaves, with five leaflets. The winged double seeds, however, are definitely of the maple family. Box elder grows throughout much of the east, in streambanks, waste places, and cities. It has become sort of a "weed tree" sprouting readily, growing quickly, and dying. It is shallow-rooted and has brittle wood. Trees growing in cities often are uprooted or damaged by summer storms. Still, this tree has some value, as it is used by amateurs to make maple sugar, and the sap can be used for wine.

In the first warm days of spring, head for the sugarbush, whether it is a woods full of stately sugar maples or a backyard "weed tree." It takes little effort to get a gallon of sap and is worth the reward.

Birches

Most of the larger species of birches can be tapped for sap, the same as maples, only a month later. Birch sap is not so sweet, but it can be used for wine in the same way.

Birches can be recognized by their peeling white, yellowish, or so-called cherry-tree bark. They also have immature "catkins" on the ends of the twigs all winter, waiting to expand and spread their pollen to the winds in spring.

Perhaps the favorite birch for sap, the sweet birch (*Betula lenta*), grows in moist woods from Maine to Kentucky. It has bark like a cherry tree and twigs with the flavor of wintergreen. Sweet birches tend to grow close together. While the sap is not very sweet, it is abundant and contains the same wintergreen flavor that is in the twigs. This species thus produces a very distinctive wine.

Another, more northern, species is the yellow birch (*Betula lutea*).

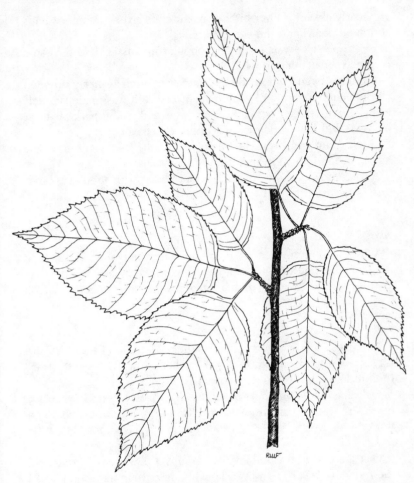

Yellow birch; *Betula lutea*

It can reach a large size in rich maple woods. Its bark tends to be a yellowish-gray and peels. The twigs also have the slight flavor of wintergreen, which will show up in the sap.

The paper birch (*Betula papyrifera*), is another northern species, found across Canada and south to New Jersey and Ohio. The Indians gathered the sap. It can be used for wine, but the wintergreen oils are nearly absent. Other birches include the river birch of swamps and flood plains and the canoe birch.

Birch sap wine was once very popular in Russia. Use the same recipe as for maple sap wine.

Birch has been used in other ways. Sweet birch formerly supplied all the commercial oil of wintergreen, before it was made synthetically. Birch tea can be made from twigs and young bark of sweet birch. It will have a degree of wintergreen flavor.

Birch syrup and sugar can be made, but the sugar content of the sap is low and much evaporation is necessary.

A well-known product of birch is birch beer, which requires birch sap, honey, and birch twigs.

TREE LEAF WINES

Wines made from tree leaves are often high in tannin, and so may need much aging to be drinkable. However, they are described as "fair to middling wines" that are good conversation pieces.

Oak

The oaks are a widespread and rather old group of trees. Of the fifty species found in North America, half grow in the east. They tend to be highly variable, freely crossbreeding.

Oaks feed large numbers of wildlife with their acorns. Most oaks, however, are not born from acorns. They sprout from the root systems of other oaks, so that a whole forest may be connected by the roots.

Oak species are divided into two groups, the white oak group and the red and black oak group. The white oak group has round-lobed leaves, without bristle tips, and includes such species as the following:

White Oak (*Quercus alba*) is a large tree of acid, well-drained soils. Its range is widespread.

Burr Oak (*Quercus macrocarpa*) is a large tree in some forests. In sand it is short, gnarled, and ugly. It can survive farther out on the prairie than most trees.

Swamp White Oak (*Quercus bicolor*) is an uncommon tree of swamps and bottomlands from Maine to Minnesota to Oklahoma.

(*Left*) white oak; *Quercus alba*; (*right*) northern red oak; *Quercus rubra*

Chestnut Oak (*Quercus muehlenbergii*) is a shrub of very dry slopes over much of the East.

The black oak group of oak species all have bristle-tipped leaves and include:

Northern Red Oak (*Quercus borealis*) a common, large tree of upland forests is a favorite of squirrels.

Scarlet Oak (*Quercus coccinea*) is a small tree found in sandy soil.

Hill's Oak (*Quercus ellipsoidalis*) is found in a limited range in the Midwest. A small tree covering many glacial sand plains with scrubby growth, it produces a heavy crop of acorns every two years.

Black Oak (*Quercus velutina*) is a widespread large tree of dry woods.

Oaks, where they grow in woods, are often used for lumber. Acorns from the white oak group are often eaten raw or with the tannins and bitterness leached out, then roasted. The bark of the oak has so much tannin in it that it was often stripped in the spring for tanning hides.

The tannin is also present in the leaves. In fall, when oak leaves have fallen, a mud puddle full of oak leaves may appear almost black from leached-out tannin. Slow-moving streams and puddles can turn brown. Tannin is the biggest problem of tree leaf wines.

To make oak leaf wine, gather a gallon of leaves as soon as they have fully leafed out, in May or June. Pour a gallon of boiling water over the leaves in a plastic pail. Add three and a half pounds of sugar and the juice of a lemon or an orange, and allow it to infuse overnight. Next day, add the wine yeast and allow to work for several days, stirring daily. Then strain into a fermentation jug and allow to ferment completely. Transfer to an aging vessel and allow to age as long as necessary, perhaps two years or more.

Experimentation would probably find that some oak leaf wines are better than others. This recipe will make a sweet wine, even if the winemaker doesn't find it too palatable.

Walnuts

The black walnut (*Juglans nigra*) was once quite abundant in its range. It was a large tree of mature forests, until its wood proved too valuable. Walnut has been used for railroad ties, cradles, and gunstocks. Lincoln split rails from black walnut to use in fences.

Because the black walnut has been ruthlessly cut down, backyard walnut trees have become very valuable. They still grow in the forests, but not in their former size or abundance.

Walnuts bear their nuts each fall, large round ones with green husks. They are eaten raw (especially at Christmas) or used to flavor ice cream. Squirrels love them.

The white walnut or butternut (*Juglans cinerea*) is somewhat less prized for its wood and so is a little more common and widespread. It differs from black walnut in that it produces larger, oblong nuts

Black walnut; *Juglans nigra*

each fall. These are often grabbed by the squirrels before they drop off the tree. Butternut is often found in moist, rich woods, river bottomlands, and streambanks.

Both species and three more of restricted range farther west have compound leaves that are feather-divided. Gather leaves from a tree growing in the open, since they will be unreachable in the woods. The same amounts and procedures used for oak leaf wine can be used to make walnut wine, though probably less aging will be needed.

For another recipe, use 150 unblemished leaves, five gallons of water, and seventeen pounds of honey. Boil for an hour, cool, then add the wine yeast. Next day, strain it into a fermentation jug and water-seal. Fermentation should take three months, then transfer to an aging jug and age.

Grape Leaves

Another wine, somewhat better, can be made from wild grape leaves and tendrils. Pick them at grape harvest time in September or, better yet, when young, in May or June. Many of the wild grape vines that never bear fruit can be used in this way.

Put five pounds of grape leaves in a plastic pail. Pour a gallon of boiling water over them. Two days later, strain off liquid, squeezing it out of the leaves. Add three pounds sugar and stir. Add wine yeast and let work open for a week, then water-seal in fermentation jug. When fermentation has ceased, transfer to an aging jug and age for one year.

WEEDS

A number of common plants that are mostly considered weeds can be used for wine. Some migrated from Europe and now make their home along roadsides and undisturbed in many places. By using them for wine, otherwise useless plants can be put to good use.

Chickweeds

Chickweeds are small, delicate, reclining plants of the carnation

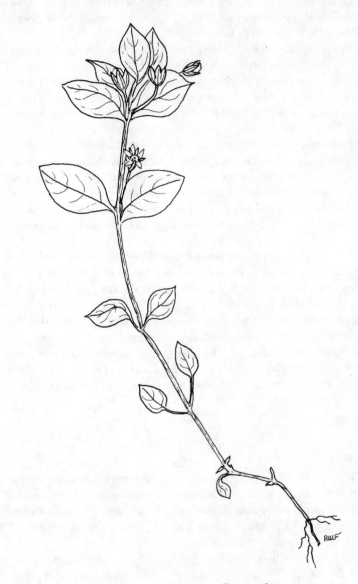

Common chickweed; *Stellaria media*

family. There are a number of species, native and imported, all in the genus *Stellaria*. They have small leaves. Their most distinguishing feature is the small white flowers, whose five petals are all deeply cleft and look like ten petals.

The species of chickweed imported from Europe is the most common in the United States. Often found growing in lawns, it grows and blooms constantly during the growing season and if it gets warm enough, in the winter. Its flowers open about midmorning. Night-flying insects are thus barred from pollinating it, although a handsome little moth in its caterpillar stage eats chickweed.

Chickweeds also are eaten by small birds, chickens, and people. The plants are eaten raw as a salad or cooked as chickweed greens.

As a medicine chickweeds have been used in poultices to treat boils and inflammations. Chickweed tea was often recommended to cure obesity. Chickweed is indeed useful in treating deficiencies in vitamin A and C. But every green vegetable can do that to various degrees.

Chickweed wine was supposedly developed by gypsies. Whether that makes it superior to other wines, the winemaker can judge. Pick a quart of chickweeds, everything but the root, any time of the year. Thinly slice the peels of a lemon and an orange and put them in a plastic pail with the clean chickweed. Pour a gallon of boiling water over them. Let this cool, and strain into another plastic pail. Add three pounds of sugar, the juices of the orange and lemon, and the wine yeast. Cover and let work for a week, stirring daily. Then siphon into a fermentation vessel and ferment to completion. Age as needed.

Angelica

The Purple Angelica (*Angelica atropurpurea*) is a huge, coarse herb of the carrot family. It is found in swamps and along stream-banks, growing taller than a man with coarse, hollow, purple stems. It ranges from Canada south to Indiana, with a couple of related species growing farther south.

The carrot family can be distinguished by its flower arrangement. Each flower cluster consists of numerous rays from a central point. At the end of each ray is another central point with more rays going out to the flowers. So the flower arrangements often look like big balls of small flowers.

Several species in the group are poisonous, especially their roots. The closely related, but smaller swamp hemlock (*Cicuta*) was Socrates' cup of hemlock. It is important to make positive identification before using this plant family.

Angelica is edible, but do not use the root. Angelica tea is said

Purple angelica; *Angelica atropurpurea*

to taste like celery. Some people boil and eat the leaves, but most people find them too bitter. Angelica seeds have been used as a substitute for juniper in flavoring gin and to flavor soft drinks, cakes, and candies.

The powdered root of European Angelica (*Angelica archangelica*) has been used to treat lung diseases and indigestion. It has been used in ear drops, eye drops, and toothache, ulcer, and gout medicine. Do not use it or any herb for self-treatment, however.

Look for angelica in July or August in an open swamp or an open meadow with a stream flowing through it. Purple Angelica is one herbaceous plant that can be seen a long distance off in these places.

When picking angelica leaves, beware of the large flower clusters. Some of the largest spiders I have ever seen make their homes in them.

Pick one-half pound of angelica leaves, which is easy to do for they are large. Carefully rinse and clean the giant spiders off them. Put them in a plastic pail. Add the peeled rinds of one lemon and one orange and their juices. Pour a gallon of boiling water over them. Next day, strain and squeeze all juice into another plastic pail. Dissolve three and one-half pounds of sugar and one package of wine yeast in the pail. Cover with cheesecloth and let stand for a week, stirring daily. Transfer to a fermentation jug and water-seal. When fermentation has completed, siphon into aging jug. Age for one year, then bottle.

Agrimony

Agrimony, the genus *Agrimonia*, is a group of half a dozen herbaceous species in the rose family. They are all herbs, about a meter tall, with long spikes of small, yellow five-petaled flowers. The species are widespread and tend to be similar. They are all found in woods, mostly moist, and can be readily recognized when they bloom in July and August.

Agrimony is listed as an herbal remedy, especially the European species (*Agrimonia eupatoria*), which is recommended for kidney stones. Made into a tea, it is suggested for use after bee stings and snake bites. Gargling agrimony is supposed to cure sore throats. Agrimony is said to improve the liver and digestive tract.

Agrimony wine is made from the stems and leaves of any species

Agrimony; *Agrimonia gryposepala*

of agrimony. Put a quart of agrimony leaves in a plastic pail. Pour
a gallon of boiling water over them. Add three pounds of sugar,
one-half ounce of ginger, and the juices and peels of one lemon and
one orange.

When cooled to room temperature, add the wine yeast. Cover
with cheesecloth and let stand for three days, stirring daily. Strain
into a fermentation jug and water-seal. Ferment to completion.
Siphon into an aging jug and age as necessary, then bottle.

Burdock

Most people have seen the disgusting weed of waste places called
burdock. In late summer and fall, the ripe fruits, called burrs, turn
brown. They stick to the clothes of a passing human and to dogs'
fur. Attempts to remove them scatter the seeds, guaranteeing a new
crop.

Burdocks are from Eurasia, and are now found throughout this
country. The Great Burdock (*Arctium lappa*) is a huge weed that
grows taller than a man in places. It is not nearly as widespread as
common burdock (*Arctium minus*), which is the one seen in most
places.

Burdocks are biennial, their first season they grow a set of leaves
at the base and no stem or flowers. Most garden root crops, including
carrots and beets, are biennial plants. Leave them in the ground
a second year and they will produce flowering stalks.

After establishing its leaves and roots, the plant stores food in the
roots for the rest of the season.

The second year, burdock sends up a branching flowering stalk
that produces the burrs. A good patch will have a lot of one year
plants, with just leaves sticking out of the ground, and some two
year plants, with flowering stalks. After producing seeds the second
year, the plant dies. Some old dead stalks will likely persist from
previous years, perhaps with burrs still attached.

As an herbal remedy, it is said to be a gentle laxative. Its roots
are used to cure rheumatism, gout, and lung conditions. In external
application, it relieves sores and swellings. A tincture made from
the seeds is said to cure psoriasis.

The Japanese have a high respect for burdock. Some consider it
an aphrodisiac. The roots at one stage are often used in sukiyaki.

Common burdock; *Arctium minus*

The peeled stems are boiled and eaten. It is treated as a green vegetable. Even the leaf stems can be eaten.

Burdock tea and burdock ale can be made, as well as a burdock wine.

Look for burdock in disturbed waste places in July or August. If you have looked all over an area and have not seen any, check your clothes for the round, green burrs. You could have missed the plant when it didn't miss you.

Gather one-half pound of the green leaves and green burrs. Clean them and throw them in a plastic pail with four pounds of *brown* sugar. Add the juice of one lemon. Pour a gallon of boiling water over it. When cooled to room temperature, add the wine yeast and allow to work for five days, stirring daily. Strain into a fermentation jug and water-seal. When fermentation has completed, siphon into an aging vessel and age as needed.

Charlock

Charlock is in the mustard family, in the genus *Brassica,* which includes cabbage, brussels sprouts, cauliflower, and broccoli. A number of wild species occupy roadsides and waste areas. They are all annual plants with yellow flowers on long stalks. The flowers all have four petals, four sepals, and six stamens inside the flower. This is characteristic of all mustard plants. Charlock (*Brassica kaber*) blooms in early summer and is about half a meter tall. Another common one, black mustard (*Brassica nigra*), grows up to one and one-half meters tall and blooms in late summer. While black mustard can be used for wine, its seeds should be avoided. The ripe seeds contain a compound which will inhibit the use of iodine by the thyroid gland, which could cause a goiter (swollen thyroid). Most members of the mustard family are entirely edible, but this is an exception.

Use an illustrated identification manual to help you differentiate weeds in the genus *Brassica,* since the mustard family is difficult to identify. Once you recognize a species, it will not be easily forgotten.

Charlock is most easily recognized at blooming season, probably in June. Gather a gallon of leaves and flowers (mostly leaves). Clean them and put them in a plastic pail with three and a half pounds

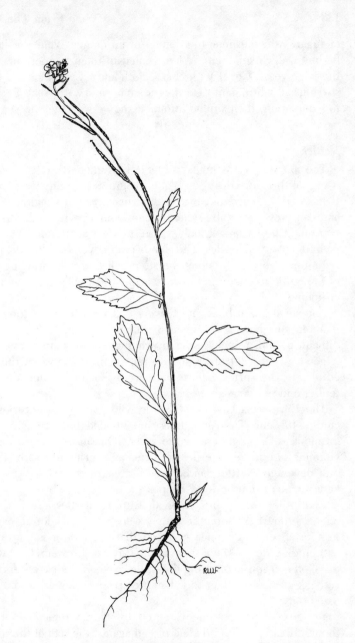

Charlock; *Brassica kaber*

of sugar. Add the juice of a lemon or an orange. Pour a gallon of boiling water over them. When cooled to room temperature, add the wine yeast. Cover with cheesecloth and let work for five days, stirring daily. Strain into a fermentation jug and water-seal. Ferment to completion, then siphon into an aging vessel. Age one year.

Nettles

The common wild stinging nettle or burning nettle (*Urtica dioica*) is one of the more despised plants. It grows in sunny waste areas. It has dark green rather oval leaves, usually with stinging bristles and can grow very tall. When forcing your way through a thicket you might find yourself looking face to stem at the top of a nettle plant or colony of nettles. The colony might even be taller than you.

Running your hand along the stem will cause the stinging hairs of the nettle to inject their formic acid, which will cause you hours of itching.

The small green buds and flowers that form near the top of the plant in summer are very small, but numerous. Nettles are not difficult to find, usually found growing where they are not wanted. A good way to control them is to put them to use when they are edible, in the spring before they are a foot high when they are tender and not yet stringy.

The Europeans have used edible wild plants for centuries, including this one. The young tops can be boiled (boiling destroys the formic acid) and eaten as nettle greens. Because they are high in vitamins and protein, nettles are taken as a spring tonic and a summer beverage. Nettles can be used for tea, or made into a beer, or an assortment of other odd recipes.

Like other wild plants eaten in Europe, nettles also have medicinal properties. Sometimes they were even considered magical. For instance, it was once believed that if a farmer got up early, gathered nettles, and fed them to the cattle before sunrise, it would drive off evil spirits plaguing the cattle. Not a bad idea, except most cattle know better than to eat nettles before they are thoroughly dried out.

Beside the usual ailments cured by herbal remedies, it was thought that a fresh nettle leaf placed against the roof of the mouth would stop a nosebleed. It seems to me that your mouth would be

Stinging nettle; *Urtica dioica*

so itchy you would forget about the nosebleed. Nettles have also been used to treat worms in children and as a treatment for stings, bites, and various plant poisonings.

With all these good things attributed to it, no wonder somebody tried to make a wine out of this disgusting weed. It is said to be lacking in character and should be flavored with something else (see herbs).

In the spring gather three quarts of young nettle tops (less than a foot tall). Clean them and put them in a plastic pail. Bruise them and add three and a half pounds of sugar and the juice of a lemon or an orange. Pour a gallon of boiling water over this. When cooled to room temperature, add the wine yeast. Cover with cheesecloth and let work for five days, stirring daily. Then strain into a fermentation jug and water-seal. Ferment to completion and age. Flavoring herbs may be either added at the beginning or infused into the finished wine.

Another nettle has been used for food and can be used for wine. This one is called the wood nettle or itchweed (*Laportea canadensis*). It is a widespread native plant of moist woods, especially river bottomlands. It is only a meter tall and can cover river bottomland forests all summer, requiring a stout heart to walk through them. Its leaves are lighter green than those of the stinging nettle, but much larger and broader. It is found throughout the eastern United States and can be used in the same ways as the stinging nettle.

Several other species of nettles are found in eastern United States, none of them the stinging variety. No evidence can be found to prove them edible or poisonous, so they are not recommended.

One of them is the false nettle (*Boehmeria cylindrica*), a small perennial herb that resembles the wood nettle, only smaller and without stinging hairs. It is found throughout the eastern United States in wet places, often on lakeshores. It is a mature plant in later summer.

The clearweed (*Pilea pumila*), is another small plant found in wet woods. It has dark green leaves, somewhat resembling stinging nettle, only smooth and shiny. It is an annual, maturing in late summer.

The pellitory (*Parietaria pensylvanica*) is a nettle of dry places. It is light colored and does not resemble other membranes of the nettle family.

Yarrow

The yarrow (*Achillea millefolium*) is a medicinal herb imported from Europe that is abundant along roadsides throughout the eastern United States. It is readily recognized as a rather aromatic green herb less than half a meter tall, with feathery, lacy leaves and large, flat-topped clusters of small white (or sometimes pink) flowers. It blooms from late June to November and may be picked anytime during this period.

Yarrow has had some quaint uses in Europe. It was often used as a love charm. If an ounce of this herb is sown into a cloth packet and placed under the pillow, you would dream of your future wife or husband. Yarrow was brought to weddings to insure that the young couple would know at least seven years of love. It was believed to be especially potent when picked from the grave of a young man.

Yarrow has been used in war to treat battle wounds. It has been used for many herbal medicine treatments. Chewing the leaves is said to cure toothache. An infusion of yarrow has been recommended for colds, measles, and fever. Washing the head with this infusion is supposed to prevent baldness. (It may not help, but won't hurt.)

Yarrow is alleged to contain small quantities of poisons, but it has long been used for yarrow tea. The Swedes have brewed beer from it. It can also be used for wine, described by Leo Zanelli in *Home Winemaking from A to Z* as "reasonable but not exciting."

Gather about half a gallon of flowering yarrow tops. Clean them and put them in a plastic pail. Add the juices of one orange and one lemon, and pour three and a half pounds of sugar over it. Pour a gallon of boiling water over this. Allow to cool to room temperature, and add the wine yeast. Cover with cheesecloth and let it work five days. Then strain into a fermentation jug and water-seal. Ferment to completion. Siphon into aging vessel and age as needed.

THE MINT FAMILY

Mints are a large family of plants found throughout the United States. Some, grown as herbs in Europe, were brought here for the same purpose and grow wild in places. Others are native plants often not used for any purpose.

All members of the mint family have some common characteristics. They have square stems, opposite leaves, and in most cases

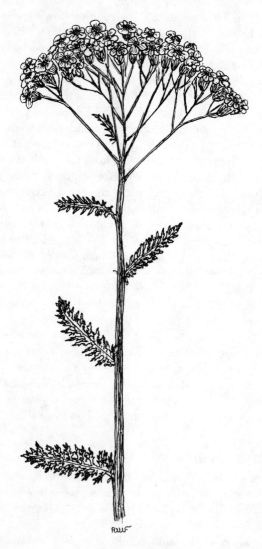

Yarrow; *Achillea millefolium*

a minty fragrance. The fragrance is unique to each species of plant, though they all will remind you of mint.

The flowers are usually small, with the petals fused into sort of a tube with upper and lower lips. The flowers are a clue to the family, but also look for other characteristics.

Nearly all members of the mint family are edible. Cases of live-stock poisoning have been attributed to a sage (*Salvia reflexa*), a hedge nettle (*Stachys arvensis*), a dead nettle (*Lamium amplexi-caule*), and ground ivy (*Glechoma hederacea*). These may have been caused by very large amounts of these plants in the diet. Most mints are quite safe, and most can be used for wine.

The same recipe can be used to make wine for any of the mints described here. Pick one-half to one gallon of mint when the plants are in bloom. It is easy to identify then and at its most aromatic. Wash the plants in cold water. Put them in a plastic pail. Pour a gallon of boiling water over them. Add three pounds of sugar and stir until dissolved. Allow to cool to room temperature and add the wine yeast. Let this mixture ferment in the open for one week, stirring three times a day. Then strain, squeeze the pulp, and place in a fermentation jug and water-seal. Allow to ferment to completion. The wine will clear readily. Siphon into wine bottles. Aging is un-necessary, but will improve the wine.

True Mints (Mentha)

The plant that is called true mint (*Mentha arvensis*) is a small plant of lakeshores, sunny swamps, and wet places throughout the temperate parts of the Northern Hemisphere. It forms patches by sending up many shoots from a common perennial plant rootstock. In July it forms small clusters of tiny pink flowers in the axils of the leaves.

Even if you fail to recognize the plant when walking through a swampy meadow, the odor of bruised plants will immediately alert you to the presence of mint. The fragrance can be readily tracked down.

My friend who goes overboard when gathering ingredients wanted to make some mint wine, so I led him to a sizable patch. He can't remember how much he picked, but recommends three or four gallons of mint to a gallon of water. This will work and produce an exceedingly minty wine, but I think the amount he actually picked was one-half to one gallon of mint. Most people probably would prefer to use much less.

Some people compare this mint wine to Peppermint Schnapps, but not as strongly flavored. It is a tasty mint beverage and a delicious after-dinner wine.

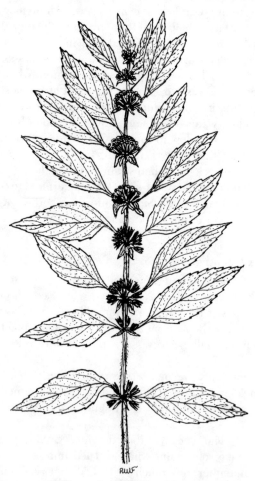

True mint; *Mentha arvensis*

Two other members of this genus are often found in wild patches. One is spearmint (*Mentha spicata*). It is used for flavoring gum, candy, mint julep, and mint jelly. Cultivated for these purposes, it also grows wild in wet places, such as streambanks. It looks similar to true mint, except the pink flowers are all at the top of the plant and the fragrance is definitely a spearmint one.

The other common *Mentha* that can be used for wine is peppermint (*Mentha piperita*). It is cultivated in herb gardens and commercially for flavoring, as in Peppermint Schnapps. It looks like spearmint, except it has longer leafstalks and a peppermint aroma.

Catnip

The little catnip mice sold as cats' toys actually contain the dry leaves of the catnip plant (*Nepeta cataria*). It is a mint with heart-shaped leaves and dense flower clusters at the top of the plant and little purple dots on the insides of the flowers. It has a most peculiar fragrance that is disagreeable to some people but loved by cats.

Catnip is a wild plant of disturbed places, especially moist ones, which blooms in late summer. Its primary use, other than to make cats make fools of themselves, is as a catnip tea. The leaves are picked and dried for this. Catnip tea is used to reduce fevers and intestinal gas. Catnip tea has been used in the treatment of scarlet fever and smallpox. Since catnip contains a mild sedative, catnip tea is useful for that purpose. It is picked anytime it is in bloom, from midsummer onward, and would likely make an interesting wine.

Wild Thyme

Wild thyme (*Thymus serpyllum*) is closely related to the garden thyme used as a seasoning. It is a garden escapee in upland woods and fields along the East Coast. It grows woody but weak square stems, with a cluster of purple mintlike flowers.

This species makes an excellent thyme-flavored honey that could be used to make a most unusual honey wine.

Wild thyme is also used as an herbal medicine in the form of tea. This tea was prescribed by the Romans for melancholia and has been recommended since then for the usual assortment of ills said to be cured by herbal medicines.

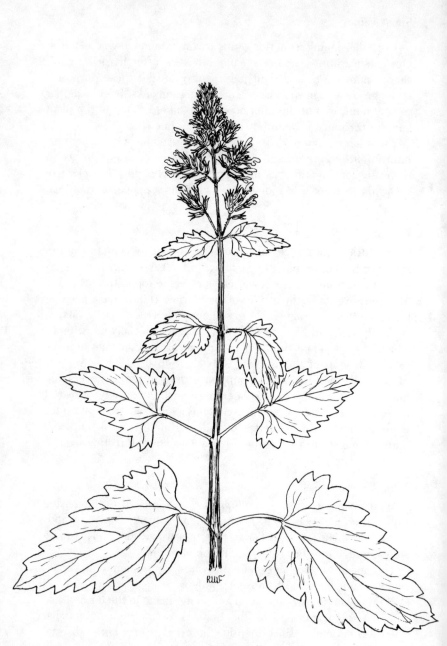

Catnip; *Nepeta cataria*

Wild thyme; *Thymus serpyllum*

If this mint were used in a wine, it would not only be a good drinking wine, but a good cooking wine, being already well-seasoned with thyme.

Wild Sage

Various species of sage, the genus *Salvia*, are found growing wild. Some of them are native plants and can be found in woods, thickets, or prairies. Others are from Europe and are found in waste places. These include the common garden sage (*Salvia officinalis*) and the clary (*Salvia sclarea*), both of which are somewhat popular in wine recipes.

Sage wine is an ancient disease preventative. Three tablespoons of sage wine every morning before breakfast, from September to March, are recommended to preserve youth and beauty.

A sage wine recipe calls for a gallon of chopped sage leaves, three pounds sugar, seven and one-half pounds of raisins, and a gallon of boiling water. Pour the water over the sage and raisins in a plastic pail. When cool to room temperature, add the wine yeast. Let work for a week, stirring twice a day. Strain into a fermentation jug and water-seal. Let ferment to completion, then age a year.

Horehound

The horehound (*Marrubium vulgare*) is well known mostly for horehound candy. It is a mint grown for its distinctive flavoring that now grows wild in many parts of the United States. It can be gathered to make a strong tea, cough syrup, or candy.

If it is used for wine, a small amount (a pint to a quart) of horehound is all that is needed, as this is strong stuff. The flavor of the leaves is the same as that of commercial horehound candy.

The flowers are small, white and mintlike. The leaves are wrinkly and covered with a white down. The plant is not at all attractive, but its flavoring oils certainly are.

Ground Ivy

The common ground ivy (*Glechoma hederacea*) while alleged to have caused poisoning in livestock, has long been used by man for many medicinal purposes. An import from Europe, it is now well established throughout much of the United States in often shady, moist and disturbed places. It is a small plant that more or less creeps along the ground. It has the standard square stems and opposing leaves of the mint family. The leaves are heart-shaped and

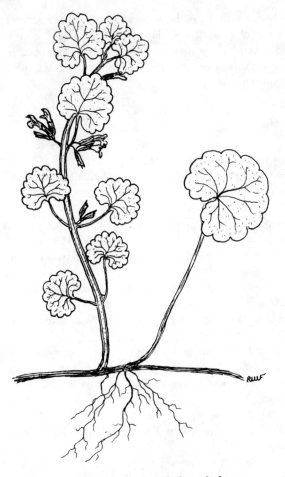

Ground ivy or creeping charlie; *Glechoma hederacea*

toothed. The flowers are bugle-shaped, mintlike, and sort of a blue-purple in odor. This plant blooms earlier than most mints, starting about mid-spring.

Ground ivy in the past has been used for a wide assortment of illnesses, and is still used for a bitter tonic and a tea. It was also once used for clarifying beer, before hops were used.

Euell Gibbons, in *Stalking the Healthful Herbs*, reported that his

Pennsylvania Dutch neighbors made a wine from ground ivy, using equal parts of ground ivy, dandelion leaves, chickory leaves, and burdock leaves. They also used the rinds of tangerines, lemons, and oranges. Because the taste is intensely bitter, this wine is intended as an appetizer only.

Other Mints

Many other mints are found in waste places and moist areas. Some of the common ones are:

Mountain mint. A dozen species of this member of the genus *Pycnanthemum*, are found in an assortment of places, more common near the East Coast and is used in tea.

Hyssop. *Hyssopus officinalis*, found in roadsides and waste places, is used in tea, soup, candy, roast meat, and stuffing.

American pennyroyal. *Hedeoma pulegioides*, widespread in upland woods, is used as a tea.

Blue giant hyssop. *Agastache foeniculum*, used in tea, is found in woods in eastern half of United States.

Wild basil. *Satureja vulgaris*, used in seasoning and tea, is widespread in upland woods.

Hedge-nettle. *Stachys palustris* and *Stachys hyssopifolia*, used as salad or cooked vegetable, is common in waste places.

Stone mint. *Cunila origanoides*, used as tea, is found in dry or rocky woods.

Henbit (*Lamium amplexicaule*) and dead nettle (*Lamium album*), leaves are cooked and eaten like spinach and can be found in waste places.

Wild marjoram. *Origanum vulgare*, used in salads, stuffings, and home remedies, can be found in disturbed places.

Self-heal. *Prunella vulgaris*, used in a cold beverage and in folk medicine, is also widespread in waste places.

Balm. *Mellissa officinalis*, used in folk medicine, escaped from cultivation and is widespread.

Beebalm or wild bergamot. *Monarda fistulosa*, used in tea, is widespread in the uplands.

Motherwort. *Leonurus cardiaca*, used as a wine herb, is widespread in waste places.

These are just a few of the many mints that one can find and make wine from. Some, grown as garden herbs in Europe, have been used in wine for centuries. Others are native to the United States and may have never been tried for wine, or else those who tried it kept it a secret. Learn to recognize all the wild mints in your vicinity, then smell them and taste them. Those whose minty smell and taste appeals to you may be usable in making excellent wine.

If there is a shortage of good wild mint locally, grow your own. Many wild mints are grown as garden herbs, and the seeds can be readily purchased. They grow easily in the garden, and if allowed to go to seed, spread easily.

TEA WINES

Wine can also be made from tea. Plants that can be made into tea can also be used for tea wine, simply by drying the leaves before making the wine. However, usually tea wines are those made from dried tea leaves of a high tannin content.

Tannin can be added to wines using teas, also. Most fruit wines have plenty of tannin. Some shoot wines do, too. Flower wines, however, are usually low in tannin. If tannin is desired, add a teaspoon or two of ordinary brewed tea to a gallon of finished wine.

Or wine can be made directly from dried tea leaves. Any commercial tea will do, or use strawberry and raspberry leaves. Pick them, spread them on newspaper in a dry place, and let them get thoroughly dry before use.

It may seem unusual to use these leaves for tea or wine, but strawberry-leaf infusion has been used in the past for a number of illnesses. It has been used as a treatment for dysentery and gout. Liver and kidney pain have been treated by a strong infusion.

Tea wine also can be made from linden trees. There are a number of European species and several native American species. The most common one is the basswood (*Tilia americana*), a characteristic tree of fertile upland woods throughout northeastern United States. It has somewhat large, rather round leaves. The flowers are white-petaled, appearing in June and July. Later, they form green fruits attached to a modified leaf, which serves as a propeller to help the fruits ride the winds and so distribute the seeds for some distance.

The odor of the basswood in flower can often be detected a mile

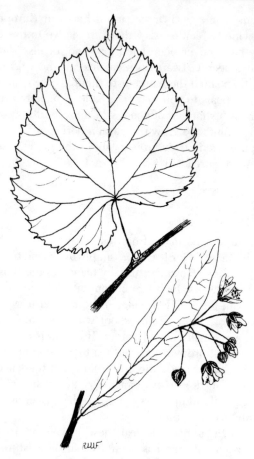

Basswood or American linden; *Tilia americana*

away. Approach a basswood tree on a sunny day and the bees, as
well as wasps, beetles, flies, and butterflies, will be quite evident.
There will no doubt be birds and spiders around to prey on the
pollinating insects. At night the basswood tree will be filled with
a great many kinds of moths, beetles, ants, as well as other strange
flying insects.

This living community will remain for about a month. There are good flows of honey from each basswood tree only two or three years out of five, but those flows make a high quality honey, sought after by all those insects, beekeepers, and honey gatherers.

It is not known if basswood flowers alone make a usable wine. I tried making a basswood candy once, but I didn't like it and neither did anyone else who wasn't trying to be polite.

Basswood flowers are used to make tea. Linden flowers have long been gathered by the French to make linden tea as herbal medicine to treat nervousness, hysteria, and insomnia.

Making Linden Tea Wine

The recipe for linden tea wine requires flowers and leaves, apparently in equal proportions. The leaves will add tannin to the mixture. Pick the flowers and leaves when the flowers are in full bloom.

Spread the flowers and leaves over a newspaper in a dry place. Let them dry completely. Most of the little bugs and spiders will crawl out on their own. When they are completely dry, you can make a tea or tea wine.

Only one ounce of the dried leaves and flowers is needed. Pour a pint of boiling water over one ounce of dried leaves and flowers and steep, as for tea. Chop a pound of raisins into a plastic pail and squeeze two lemons into it. Grate the rinds of the lemons and add those. Strain the tea into the plastic pail and add enough hot water to make a gallon. Add three pounds of sugar and dissolve completely. When lukewarm, add the wine yeast and cover with cheesecloth. Let it work for a week, stirring daily. Strain into a fermentation vessel and water-seal. Ferment to completion. Siphon into an aging vessel. Bottle when it is clear and age.

This recipe can be used on basswood, strawberry, and raspberry leaf tea. Those with a lot of tannin will need more aging than those with less.

HERBS

Many herbs are used in home winemaking. Many of them do not grow wild in this country. Others are native or introduced wild plants, which can be gathered readily by a determined winemaker.

Herbs are sometimes added to the plastic pail at the beginning of the winemaking process. Many recipes, for instance, call for the addition of small amounts of ginger. Other herbs are used to flavor finished wines by suspending a bag of herbs in the wine and letting the flavoring infuse into the wine. A single kind of herb may be used, or a combination of them. The leaves, flowers, and roots of herbs can be used.

Mints

As previously discussed, all members of the mint family can be used to infuse other wines. The choice is left to the winemaker, who will prefer the fragrance of some mints over others.

Those that are often used for herb wines include spearmint (genus *Mentha*) and motherwort (*Leonurus cardiaca*). The variety of possibilities, however, is considerable.

Tansy

The tansy (*Tanacetum vulgare*) is a common perennial herb that forms large colonies. It has very aromatic foliage of dark-green, lacy leaves. The flowers are in flat-topped clusters of yellow heads, which can be seen from June to November. This is a widespread introduced weed.

This plant is a medicinal herb used to destroy worms and as a tonic, to aid digestion and relieve back pains.

Some winemaking books also suggest its use to add bitterness to wines. The amount of bitterness desired determines the amount needed. A word of caution, however, too much tansy-induced bitterness could be fatal. Overdoses of the oils of this plant, when used as medicine, have killed people. Therefore, I do not recommend the use of this plant for wine or medicine.

Goldenrod

All species of goldenrod could be used, but the one most likely to be effective is the sweet goldenrod (*Solidago odora*) used for tea because of its fragrant leaves.

Pansies and Violets

The flowers of the cultivated pansy (*Viola tricolor*) are listed as a wine herb. They sometimes escape from cultivation and may be used as a wild plant. Any other species of violet or pansy can also be used.

Yarrow

Previously discussed under Weed Wines, the fragrant foliage may be used as an herbal flavoring in another wine.

Sweet Flag

The sweet flag (*Acorus calamus*) is a common plant of swamps and marshes, found in America and Eurasia. It looks like cattails, except it is smaller and grows in smaller patches. It is easiest to identify when it blooms in early summer. On some of the leaf-like stems a small yellow spike protrudes at an angle. This is the flower cluster. The plant can be harvested when it is flowering or any other time.

All parts of the plant are sweet and aromatic. Young leaves may be gathered for a salad, but the root is the most desirable part.

Just under the mud, the root, actually an underground stem or rhizome, turns horizontal and is easy to dig out. This root has long been a cure-all to Europeans and American Indians. It has been used for a candy.

For wine, dig up some sweet flag and wash and dry it thoroughly. Grate it, and infuse the gratings into a finished wine. But don't use too much—a little goes a long way.

Speedwell

The common speedwell (*Veronica officinalis*) is another species listed as a wine herb. There are over a dozen species of speedwells in northeastern United States. All are members of the snapdragon family in the genus *Veronica*. They are all low herbs, sprawling or barely rising off the ground. They have small blue flowers with the petals fused together. The flowers have three rounded lobes that

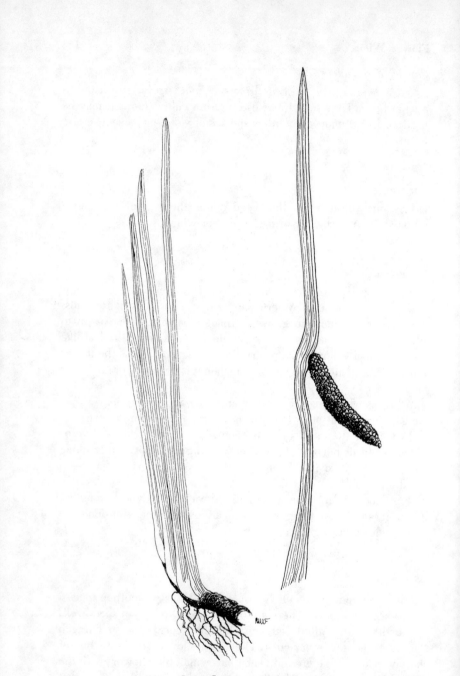

Sweet flag; *Acorus calamus*

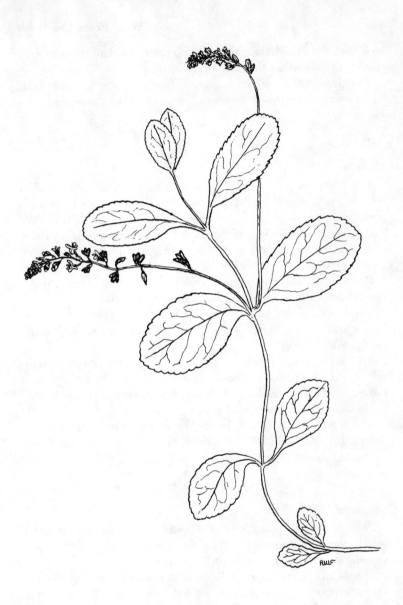

Speedwell; *Veronica officinalis*

look alike and a fourth lobe that is much narrower. This characteristic is what distinguishes the speedwells.

They have flowers all season, mostly few flowers on any one plant. The common speedwell, however, has a lot of flowers when in full bloom.

Mullein

The common mullein (*Verbascum thapsus*), also called Indian tobacco, is a common weed of roadsides, disturbed areas, and especially pastures. It grows towering spikes of yellow flowers, two meters or more tall. The mullein is a biennial, producing a rosette of leaves at the base the first year, surviving the winter, growing its flower stalk the second year, after which it dies.

It is a weed introduced from Europe, which has become widespread, sometimes almost taking over pasturelands.

The leaves of this plant are covered with soft, velvety hair. The flower spikes, at the top of the plant, are unbranched with many small yellow flowers.

Mullein leaves and flowers have been used in many a home remedy, especially cough medicine. There are many other unproven claims for its medicinal use. It is listed as a wine herb, containing some volatile oils, gums, and resins.

The leaves, if used, can be gathered from first year plants or during the winter and used fresh or dried. Flowers must be gathered fresh, in July or August.

Shepherd's Purse

The common shepherd's purse (*Capsella bursa-pastoris*) is a very weedy member of the mustard family. It is an entirely edible plant, sometimes used as a wine herb.

Shepherd's purse is a small herb, with numerous deeply divided, almost compound, leaves growing out of its base. It sends up a flowering stalk with white flowers and small, green, heart-shaped, flattened pods.

Look for the weed in any weedy place, including lawns and gardens.

Mullein; *Verbascum thapsis*

St. John's-Wort

St. John's-Wort (*Hypericum perforatum*) is a very common road-side weed, imported from Europe. It is a summer-blooming plant with large clusters of bright yellow flowers. Its small, oblong leaves, when held up to the light, show small red dots, or glands. These

St. John's Wort; *Hypericum perforatum*

dots are said to appear every August 29 when John the Baptist was beheaded, hence the plant's name. A ridge runs down the stem below each leaf.

This herb has been used as a nerve medicine in ancient herbal practices and to treat sores and external wounds.

It also contains a mild poison, a fluorescent pigment, that reacts to light. This poison is not broken down by the liver, but settles in the skin, making the skin quite sensitive to light. It is not often fatal but can be uncomfortable. If St. John's-Wort is used as a wine herb, the amount used should be limited.

Chicory

A common roadside weed is chicory (*Cichorium intybus*). It grows flowering stalks in early summer, a meter or less tall. The stalks are branched and produce numerous blue flowers, somewhat like the dandelion, but with wider petals that are toothed at the ends. The flowers are not always open, but a roadside covered with them is a pretty sight when they are.

Being related to the dandelion, chicory is used in similar ways. The early spring foliage is eaten as salad greens. The dried root is used to make a brew somewhat stronger than coffee. Perhaps the flowers could make a good wine by themselves. But it is the roots that are used as wine flavoring. They are long taproots that are dug, cleaned, and dried.

Wild Caraway

The wild caraway (*Carum carvi*) is the same species that caraway seeds are harvested from in cultivation. It is a plant less than a meter tall, with finely divided, lacy leaves. The flowers, which appear in June, are very small and white, in a formation typical of the carrot family. They are five-petaled and produce a nectar very attractive to bees, who produce a valuable honey.

This plant is another European plant that escaped from cultivation and established itself along roadsides across southern Canada and south to Virginia and Missouri. In places, miles of roadside may be covered with this delicate herb. It is a biennial, producing leaves from the base the first year and a flowering stalk the second.

Chicory; *Cichorium intybus*

Wild caraway; *Carum carvi*

The mature caraway seeds are the parts used. Look for them in late July or August. They can easily be shaken from the tops when ripe. An ounce of caraway seeds (at most) is used to flavor other wines, usually flower wines. They may be added at the start of the winemaking process or as an infusion at the end.

Caraway seeds can be dried and stored for long periods and used for any other cooking purpose that calls for caraway, as well as wine.

While most of the wild herbs that can be used as wine-flavoring herbs have been listed, there are others that may be only very local escapees from nearby gardens. There may be others that are native plants of only limited distribution. Also, in different areas people have learned different uses for local native plants, and some popular local herb or seasoning may be tried as a wine herb. If there are no wild ones in your area that can be used for any such purpose, there's always the seed catalog. Many kinds will become established as wild plants if the seeds fall in the right place.

Chapter Six

Root Wines

Roots for winemaking include all plants that must be dug up to reach the main ingredient. It includes roots, but may also include corms, bulbs, tubers, or rhizomes, all modified stems, or parts thereof. Defining everything that must be dug out of the ground as roots saves a lot of unnecessary technical trouble.

One problem with using roots for winemaking (beside getting them clean) is starch. Roots are the food storage systems of plants. The sugars transferred down to the roots for storage are converted into starches, which are much longer and more stable molecules.

Poorer quality yeasts often have trouble digesting the starches in root wines and the starches remain to form a hazy wine with a starchy taste. This problem can be cured in most cases by always using wine yeast. In some cases, leaving the roots in the ground until a frost occurs will increase the sugar content. This is practical in gardens where you can mark the plants, but wild plants are difficult to identify when their shoots have died back. Wild roots should therefore be gathered any time they can be identified.

There are relatively few wild plants whose roots can be dug for wine, but a fair number of garden plants. Beets, parsnips, carrots, potatoes, and turnips are all used. Beets and carrots should be picked when the roots are still small and sweet. Potatoes should be dug after the plants have died down and kept in a cool, dark place for awhile before being used. Parsnips and turnips should be left in the ground until frost.

Because there are so few root wines to try, a recipe for a common cultivated root wine, beet wine, is given. It produces an excellent wine that doesn't waste the beets.

Making Beet Wine

Peel and wash four pounds of small, tender beets. Boil them in enough water to cover them for one hour. Then, strain off the juice into a plastic pail and eat the beets. Add enough water to the beet juice and three pounds of sugar to make one gallon. When lukewarm, add the wine yeast. Allow to ferment for a week, then transfer into a fermentation jug and water-seal. When fermentation has ceased and the wine clears, siphon it into an aging vessel. Age at least one year. Do not try to sample this wine any sooner than a year. It takes time.

WILD ONIONS

An assortment of almost a dozen species of wild garlics, leeks, and onions grow in the fields, woods, and prairies of the United States. They can be used for food in the same way as cultivated onions, though they are smaller and sometimes stronger.

Onion wine can be made, though it may sound rather disagreeable.

The wild leek (*Allium tri coccum*) is found in moist, rich woods from New England to Minnesota and south to Tennessee. It provides some of the first spring green to the forest floor. When the spring flowers are blooming, wild leeks send up broad, flat leaves. Since they grow in colonies, they form dense clusters. They can be identified by crinkling the leaves and sniffing them. The strong odor of onion will be unmistakable. The leaves of wild leek remain all spring

Wild leek; *Allium tricoccum*

until the trees overhead leaf out. Then the leaves die back completely, and the bulbs send up short flower stalks, about fifteen centimeters high, with rather colorless greenish-white flowers. The flower stalks die in the fall, but remain, marking where the bulb is.

The bulb can be picked anytime but it is more enjoyable to do so in the spring, when spring flowers, butterflies, and green foliage gladden the heart. The bulbs are easy to dig with a trowel. Thinning out the patches, rather than digging up a whole patch, will improve the crop next year.

Making Wild Onion Wine

Gather about two cups of wild leeks. Clean them and remove the leaves and roots. Put them in a plastic pail. Add a gallon of boiling water and three pounds of sugar and stir. When cooled to room temperature, add the wine yeast. Cover with a cheesecloth and allow to work. Because this mixture smells very strongly of onion, allow this wine to work in an out-of-the-way area.

Strain the liquid into a fermentation jug and water-seal. When fermenting is complete, bottle and age for a year or so.

It is not too drinkable as a dessert wine, but does make a good white cooking wine.

WILD GINGER

The wild ginger (*Asarum canadense*) is an interesting plant of spring woodlands found in northeast United States and southeast Canada.

The roots are shallow, horizontal, and about a centimeter thick. At the end of each root a pair of leaves sprouts. They are heart-shaped, dark green leaves, covered with soft, white velvety hairs. In between the leaves, inconspicuous and close to the ground, is the flower. It has three fused, purple-brown petals with whiplike tails on the ends. It has a cuplike shape.

This plant often forms colonies in the woods, and the rhizomes or roots can be easily dug in a colony.

Wild ginger is not related to the commercial ginger plant, but was once used as a mild substitute for it. The Indians used it for

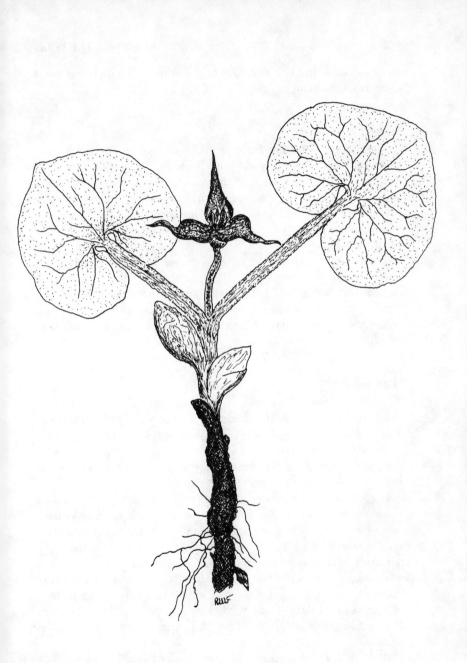

Wild ginger; *Asarum canadense*

flavoring. It is used to make tea and can be candied. It has been used as a whooping cough remedy.

Making Wild Ginger Wine

Many wine recipes call for the addition of small amounts of ginger, and wild ginger can be readily substituted.

To use wild ginger, dig out the roots in the spring. Wash them and allow them to dry thoroughly. Before adding the dried ginger roots to the wine mix, bruise them up thoroughly. Otherwise, for wine, use fresh roots and cut them into small pieces. Bruise the fresh roots also.

There are an assortment of ginger wine recipes as well, using ginger as the main ingredient. Use the standard winemaking procedure with an ounce of fresh wild ginger roots, the juice of two lemons, three and a half pounds of sugar, and a gallon of water. The completely fermented wine should be allowed to age for about three months.

Wild Carrot

Here and there along roadsides and in waste areas, you can find the common Queen Anne's Lace (*Daucus carota*) in bloom in July. This is actually the wild carrot, the same species grown in gardens and sold in supermarkets. The wild carrot has gone wild, so its roots, instead of being large and orange, are small and white. They taste like cultivated carrots, though not as sweet.

Carrots are biennial, storing food in the roots the first year and blooming the second. To see what Queen Anne's Lace looks like, leave a few carrots in the garden for a second year. They will send up a flower stalk with a dense cluster of white flowers at the top.

Carrot wine can be made from wild carrots, but it takes a lot. They are best gathered late in their first year, so look for flowering plants, then dig the first year roots out. It takes about five pounds of carrots to a gallon of water. Simmer these about fifteen minutes before using the standard recipe. A half pound of raisins can be added.

It is much easier to use cultivated carrots for this wine, but the wild carrots are free.

Wild carrot roots, foliage, and seeds have been used as herbal medicines, alleged to cure a wide variety of complaints. An infusion of the foliage is said to cure a number of internal ills. The roots, boiled until tender, are used for poultices to treat skin infections. The seeds, made into a tea, treat many things, including hiccups and chronic coughs.

The seeds can be used as a wine-flavoring herb. Gather them from the flowering tops in later summer or early fall. An ounce of seeds can be used as an infusion to flavor wine. Put them in a small cloth sack with or without other herbs and suspend them in a finished wine.

Chapter Seven

Other Possibilities

This book includes many of the wild plants of the United States that have been made into wine. In many cases the recipes are only a matter of substituting wild fruit for domestic varieties in standard recipes. This does not mean that these wild plants are the only ones that can be tried for wine. A lot of other plants or plant parts are safe to eat and can be used as experimental wine recipes. While all prospects could not possibly be included, the most likely ones are discussed.

APPLE BLOSSOMS

Like the flowers of roses, meadowsweets, and hawthorns, many other members of the rose family produce fragrant flowers in abundance, which could be made into wine. The wild apple is a particularly good example. Find the tree in the apple patch with the most fragrant flowers. When in full bloom, pick a half gallon of the flowers.

Put the flowers in a plastic pail. Pour a gallon of hot or cold water over them. Add the juices of one lemon and one orange and three and a half pounds of sugar. When the mixture is at room temperature, add the wine yeast. Stir thoroughly. Cover with cheesecloth and let stand for two weeks, stirring daily. Strain into a fermentation vessel and water-seal. Allow to ferment to completion, then sample. If aging is required, siphon to an aging vessel and let stand for up to one year. This recipe may work for the fragrant flowers of plums and cherries as well.

COMFREY

Comfrey has been given more praise by ancient and modern herbalists than most herbs. It apparently has such curative powers that it is sometimes cultivated in this country for that purpose.

Comfrey (*Symphytum officinale*) is an herb of the borage family, introduced from Europe. Less than a meter tall, it has large, coarse, hairy leaves that seem to run down the sides of the stem. It has curled clusters of bell-shaped flowers in variable colors. In one patch I found next to a trout stream, the plants had blue flowers, except one plant with white ones. Another patch, growing miles away in a wet ditch, had pink flowers.

Like other wild plants, comfrey has had many medicinal uses. Research has proved the ancient herbalists correct about comfrey's medicinal value—the roots do contain a compound actually prescribed to treat ulcers.

The young leaves of early spring comfrey can be made into a tea or eaten fresh. The roots can be made into a decoction or into a coffee.

Making Comfrey Wine

To make comfrey wine it would be necessary to dig, clean, and peel the roots and split them lengthwise. If I were to invent a recipe, I would use a quart of roots, three and one-half pounds of sugar, the juices of one lemon and one orange, and one-half pound of raisins.

Comfrey; *Symphytum officinale*

Treat this plant with respect where it is found. If you dig up roots, leave at least half, so the plant can reseed itself.

WILD RICE

Wild rice is a plant of slowly flowing, unpolluted water found across eastern United States and Canada. It is an annual plant of the grass family and grows in water up to a meter deep.

There are three varieties of wild rice. The eastern variety can grow up to three meters tall. Two others, found in the midwest and north, are smaller. The northern variety, found in Canada and the upper Midwest, was and is an important food source for the Ojibwa Indians. It was gathered from the rice fields in late summer by knocking it off the heads into the canoes. On shore, it was dried and pounded.

Today there are attempts to cultivate wild rice on Indian reservations, since wild rice brings a high price commercially. It is also still found growing wild in many places.

Look for wild rice in flowages, a lake with a small stream flowing through it (hence a little current), and slow-moving rivers. Rice usually grows in patches, sometimes covering many acres. It is a grass with separate male and female spikelets at the top. The male spikelets are loose and spreading and are below the female spikelets, which produce the wild rice.

Once found, watch the rice field until enough of the grains mature. In some lakes in northern Wisconsin, there is a posted wild rice season, usually one day, during which the rice can be gathered. These lakes have an abundance of wild rice, so everyone who may want to harvest it can get an equal chance. Enough wild rice grains fall into the water by wild rice season to insure a crop the next year. Wild rice must reseed itself each year.

Many smaller wild rice patches are not so regulated and can be harvested any time. Remember to leave enough for seed. Harvesting is done in late summer.

Making Wild Rice Wine

Though no recipes for wild rice wine are available, wild rice could be substituted for cultivated rice in saki, rice wine. Try combining three pounds of wild rice, three pounds of sugar, a pound of raisings, the juice of one lemon, and a gallon of boiling water. When this cools to room temperature, add the wine yeast. Cover with cheese-cloth and allow it to work to completion, stirring daily. Strain the liquid into a fermentation jug and water-seal. When the bubbles have ceased, carefully siphon into wine bottles. Cork the bottles and allow the wine to age for six months.

SUMAC

Sumacs are shrubs about two to three meters tall which grow in groups in dry places. They are related to poison ivy, poison oak, and poison sumac. The difference is that poison ones produce poisonous white fruits and the others produce nonpoisonous red fruits.

There are a number of species of red-fruited sumacs. Most have long compound leaves with many leaflets. All are widespread.

The staghorn sumac (*Rhus typhina*) can be distinguished by its branches, which are covered with hairs, resembling the tines of a deer's antlers. The smooth sumac (*Rhus glabra*) looks similar but with smooth, hairless branches. The winged sumac (*Rhus copallina*) has little wings of leaves along the leaf stem. It blooms later than the other two and tends to be shorter.

Making Sumac Wine

All three species produce striking red foliage in early fall. Their red fruits can be gathered at this time or earlier. The fruiting clusters should be gathered when red and in any quantity. Lightly wash the fruit to remove dust and bugs if necessary. Then put them in a container, cover them with water, and mash them up with a hand potato masher. Then strain the juice through cheesecloth to remove plant hairs and bugs. This *Rhus* juice can be sweetened with sugar to form a somewhat acid drink like lemonade.

This tasty concoction could just as well be fermented as is. No lemon juice would be needed, since it is acid already. Try using about five pounds of sumac clusters and three and one-half pounds of sugar to a gallon of water. Hot water would be unnecessary, though a campden tablet may be desirable to kill off any wild yeast disturbing the brew. Add the wine yeast and allow it to work to

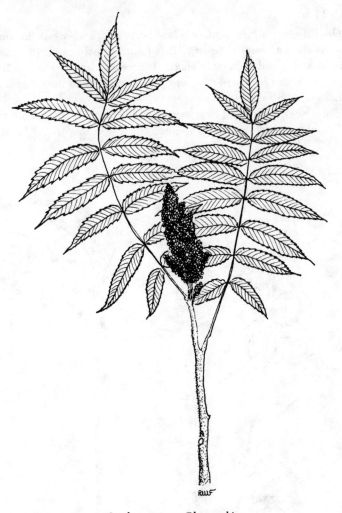

Staghorn sumac; *Rhus typhina*

completion, stirring daily. Strain into a fermentation jug and water-seal. When the bubbles have ceased, siphon into wine bottles. Cork and age the wine.

Some of the *Rhus* juice could be fermented; some of it could be consumed as a *Rhus*-ade; and some used in jelly.

WINTERGREEN

The little wintergreen plant (*Gaultheria procumbens*) is, in some dry woods, an abundant plant. It is found mostly in northeastern United States and adjacent Canada. It grows to several centimeters high, blooms in July, and develops red berries late in the fall, which remain all winter.

The newer leaves and berries are eaten freely by many animals, and hunters and hikers help themselves to the leaves and berries

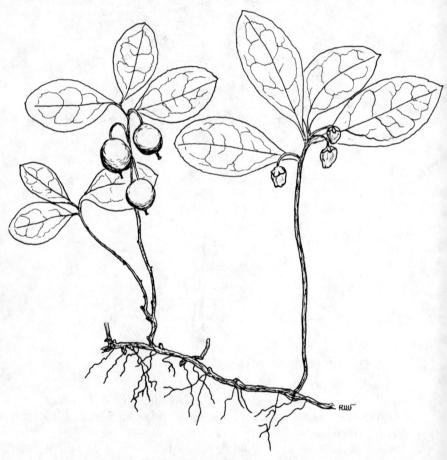

Wintergreen; *Gaultheria procumbens*

as well. The red berries can be eaten or made into a pie. They can be picked either in the fall or in the spring, when they are said to be better tasting.

The berries and leaves contain wintergreen oil. Fresh leaves contain relatively little but it comes out after a couple of days of fermentation in a sealed jar.

Making Wintergreen Wine

Perhaps the berries can be made into a wine. The new leaves of the year apparently can be. Euell Gibbons tried a recipe borrowed from his Pennsylvania Dutch neighbors using new red leaves of wintergreen, but green leaves also could be used.

Pick a half gallon of new wintergreen leaves. (New ones are lighter colored than old ones.) Pour a half gallon of boiling water over them in a plastic pail. Next day, strain off the liquid and save it. Pour another half gallon of boiling water over the leaves to get out all essential oils. When lukewarm, pour the other half gallon back in. Add four pounds of honey or three pounds of sugar. Add wine yeast and cover with cheesecloth, stirring daily for a week. Then siphon into a fermentation jug, water-seal, and ferment to completion. Age for three to six months.

GROUND CHERRY

Ground cherries (*Physalis*) are an assortment of weedy plants that are related to tomatoes. They are widespread but often local or rare. Some species are better tasting than others.

They all have drooping, bell-shaped flowers. The fruits are surrounded by a papery cover. When ripe the fruits look like little yellow tomatoes and have a sweet taste.

Ground cherries tend to grow in dry places, usually in patches. They ripen in late summer or early fall. The ripe fruits, enclosed in their dried brown calyx, often drop to the ground when they are ripe.

Ground cherries can be made into pies and preserves. In fact, one variety is sold by seed companies as a garden vegetable. Another variety, with bright red fruits, is sold for flower gardens under the name Chinese Lantern.

Ground cherry; *Physalis virginiana*

If these fruits are available and taste good to you, try them for wine. If they don't work, you can always eat ground cherry pie.

INDIAN POTATO OR GROUNDNUT

The Indian potato (*Apios americana*) is a twining legume plant found in moist thickets and woods. It is found through much of northeastern United States.

The Indian potato twines around anything handy. It has compound leaves with five leaflets. The flowers are maroon and occur in clusters. Like most members of the legume family, the flowers have the peculiar bean- and pea-flower shape. They are very attractive and fragrant to bees.

If one finds a sunny thicket with Indian potatoes twining all over, follow the stems down to the ground and dig. A few centimeters down, there will be a tuber, about ten centimeters across. Several stems may grow out of one tuber.

This is the potato that was eaten by many Indian tribes for centuries. It is said to be one of the best wild foods. It was once said that if civilization had started in the range of the Indian potato, it would have been the first tuber cultivated.

The pilgrims in their first hard winter supposedly lived on these tubers. The small Swedish colony that once existed on the Delaware River ate them when it ran out of bread. They are good in an emergency or even anytime.

Making Indian Potato Wine

The Indian potato tubers could be tried in a potato wine recipe. Put three pounds of washed tubers, a pound of raisins, and four pounds of sugar in a pail. Pour in a gallon of boiling water. When this cools to room temperature, add the wine yeast. Cover with cheesecloth and allow it to work to completion, stirring daily. Strain the liquid into a fermentation jug and water-seal. When the bubbles have ceased, carefully siphon into wine bottles. Cork the bottles and allow the wine to age for six months.

JERUSALEM ARTICHOKE

The Jerusalem artichoke (*Helianthus tuberosus*) is a native Amer-

Groundnut or Indian potato; Apios americana

ican species of sunflower. It is a common and widespread plant, growing two meters or more tall. The plants are covered with yellow flowers in late summer.

Jerusalem Artichokes grow in dense clusters along roadsides and in fields. In their roots are large numbers of tubers, which are dug after the first frost. The tubers are prepared and eaten the same way as potatoes, except that they are free. They can also be cultivated for their tubers, as well as their bright flowers.

The tubers of this plant might also be used in a potato wine recipe.

List of Wine Species

This list is made from using the Gleason and Cronquist *Manual of Vascular Plants of the Northeastern United States*. The book covers the area from Maine to Minnesota to Missouri to Virginia and adjacent parts of southern Canada. The entries are listed scientific name first, followed by a common name, if there is one. Some plants have many common names, differing from place to place, which is why the scientific name is important.

Species not generally used as wine ingredients are excluded from this list.

Lilliaceae—lily family
genus *Allium*–onion
    Allium tricoccum–wild leek
    Allium vineale–scallions
    Allium schoenoprasum
    Allium canadense
    Six more in genus

Juglandaceae—walnut family
genus *Juglans*
    Juglans cinerea–butternut
    Juglans nigra–black walnut

Betulaceae—birch family
genus *Betula*
    Betula lutea—yellow birch
    Betula lenta–sweet birch
    Betula nigra–river birch
    Betula papyrifera–paper birch
    Betula cordifolia–canoe birch

Fagaceae—beech family
genus *Quercus*–oaks
    Quercus alba–white oak
    Quercus macrocarpa–bur oak
    Quercus bicolor–swamp white oak
    Quercus borealis–northern red oak
    Quercus coccinea–scarlet oak
    Twenty more in area

Moraceae—mulberry family
genus *Humulus*
    Humulus lupulus–hops
    Humulus japonicus–Japanese hops

Urticaceae—nettles family
    Laportea canadensis–wood nettles
    Urtica dioica–stinging nettles

Aristolochiaceae–birthwort family
    Asarum canadense–wild ginger

Caryophyllaceae—carnation family
    Stellaria–chickweed
    Stellaria media
    Thirteen more species in area, less common

Ranunculaceae—buttercup family
    Caltha palustris–cowslip

Cruciferae—mustard family
genus *Brassica*
    Brassica kaber–charlock
    Brassica nigra–black mustard
    Brassica juncea–brown mustard
    Two more in area

Saxifragaceae–saxifrage family
genus *Ribes*–gooseberries and currants
    Ribes missouriense–Missouri gooseberry
    Ribes cynosbati–prickly gooseberry
    Ribes oxyacanthoides
    Ribes setosum
    Ribes lacustre–swamp black currant
    Ribes nigrum–black currant
    Ribes triste–swamp red currant
    Eight others in area

Rosaceae—rose family
genus *Spiraea*
    Spiraea alba–white meadowsweet
    Spiraea latifolia–meadowsweet
    Spiraea tomentosa–hardhack
    Spiraea japonica–Japanese lilac
    Three others in area

genus *Fragaria*–strawberries
    Fragaria vesca–Carolina strawberry
    Frageria virginiana–Virginia strawberry

genus *Rubus*–blackberries and raspberries
    Rubus strigosus–raspberry
    Rubus occidentalis–black raspberry
    Rubus parviflorus–thimbleberry
    Rubus acaulis–arctic raspberry
    Rubus–numerous blackberries and dewberries;
twenty-four species of *Rubus* listed in area

genus *Agrimonia*–agrimony
 Agrimonia gryposepala
 Six others in area

genus *Rosa*–roses
 Rosa carolina–Carolina rose
 Rosa palustris–swamp rose
 Rosa acicularis–prickly wild rose
 Rosa blanda–smooth wild rose
 Fifteen more listed in this area, many escaped from
 cultivation

genus *Prunus*–plums and cherries
 Prunus pumila–sand cherry
 Prunus serotina–black cherry
 Prunus virginiana–choke cherry
 Prunus pennsylvanica–pin cherry
 Prunus americana–American plum
 Prunus maritima–beach plum
 Prunus angustifolia–chicksaw plum
 Prunus munsoniana–wild goose plum
 Prunus hortulana–wild plum
 Prunus nigra–canadian plum
 Ten more in area, some escaped from cultivation

genus *Pyrus*–apples
 Pyrus malus–apple
 Pyrus ioensis–Iowa crabapple
 Pyrus coronaria–crabapple
 Pyrus angustifolia–crabapple

genus *Sorbus*–mountain ash
 Sorbus americana
 Sorbus decora
 Sorbus aucuparia
 The last one is cultivated and sometimes escapes

genus *Crataegus*–hawthorns
 Twenty-one species listed in area. Very difficult to
 differentiate.

genus *Amelanchier*–juneberries
    Amelanchier laevis–juneberry
    Amelanchier arborea–downy serviceberry
    Amelanchier canadensis
    Amelanchier spicata
    Four more in area

Fabaceae—bean family
genus *Trifolium*–clovers
    Trifolium pratense–red clover
    Trifolium hybridum–alsike clover
    Trifolium repens–white clover
    Fourteen more clovers listed in area.

Aceraceae—maple family
genus *Acer*
    Acer saccharum–sugar maple
    Acer nigrum–black maple
    Acer rubrum–red maple
    Acer saccharinum–soft maple
    Acer negundo–box elder

Vitaceae—grape family
genus *Vitis*
    Vitis rotundifolia–Muscadine grape
    Vitis labrusca–fox grape
    Vitis riparia–riverbank grape
    Vitis vulpina–forest grape
    Six others in area

Tiliaceae—linden family
genus *Tilia*
    Tilia americana–basswood
    Tilia heterophylla
    Tilia monticola

Violaceae—violet family
genus *Viola*
    Viola pedata–bird's foot violet

Viola papilionacea–butterfly violet
Viola sororia–wooly blue violet
Viola cucullata–marsh violet
Viola odorata–sweet violet
Viola palustris–northern marsh-violet
Viola pubescens–downy yellow violet
Viola canadensis–Canada violet
Viola arvensis–field pansy
Viola adunca–sand violet
Forty-one other species in area

Cactaceae—cactus family
genus *Opuntia*
   Opuntia compressa–prickly pear

Umbelliferae—carrot family
   Daucus carota–wild carrot
   Angelica atropurpurea–purple angelica
   Angelica venenosa
   Angelica triquinata

Ericaceae—heath family
   Gaultheria procumbens–wintergreen
genus *Vaccinium*–cranberries and blueberries
   Vaccinium oxycoccos–small cranberry
   Vaccinium vitis-idaea–mountain cranberry
   Vaccinium macrocarpon–cranberry
   Vaccinium angustifolium–blueberry
   Vaccinium corymbosum–swamp blueberry
   Vaccinium myrtilloides–velvet blueberry
   Twenty-one more species in area, mostly blueberries

Verbenaceae—vervain family
genus *Verbena*–vervain
   Verbena urticifolia
   Verbena hastata
   Verbena stricta
   Verbena simplex
   Seven more in area

Labiatae—mint family
    Marrubium vulgare–horehound
    Nepeta cataria–catnip
    Glechoma hederacea–ground ivy
    Salvia officinalis–garden sage
    Thymus serpyllum–wild thyme
    Mentha arvensis–true mint
    Mentha spicata–spearmint
    Mentha piperita–peppermint
    Thirty-four other genera listed in area, and over a hundred
    other species

Caprifoliaceae—honeysuckle family
genus *Sambucus*–elder
    Sambucus canadensis–common elder
    Other species in western states

genus *Lonicera*–honeysuckles
    Lonicera tatarica–Tartarian honeysuckle
    Lonicera canadensis–fly honeysuckle
    Lonicera dioica–wild honeysuckle
    Nine more listed in area

Compositae—daisy family
    Anthemis nobilis–chamomile, Roman chamomile
    Matricaria chamomilla–wild chamomile, German chamomile
    Achillea millefolium–yarrow
    Chrysanthemum leucanthemum–daisy, ox-eye daisy

genus *Arctum*–burdock
    Arctium minus–common burdock
    Arctium lappa–great burdock
    One more in area

genus *Taraxacum*–dandelions
    Taraxacum officinale–dandelion
    Two others in area—much less common

Bibliography

While this book should be adequate for those with a knowledge of some wild plants and little interest in the more technical aspects of home winemaking, most people will need identification manuals. Other wine books are more technical with their winemaking and contain additional recipes.

FORAGING AND HERBAL MEDICINE BOOKS

Densmore, Frances, "44th Report of the Bureau of American Ethnology," 1926–27, pp. 285–397.

An exhaustive study of the uses of plants for all purposes by the Chippewa Indians in northern Minnesota.

Gibbons, Euell, *Beachcombers Handbook,* New York: David McKay Co., 1972.

Gibbons spent three years during the 1940s in Hawaii living off the land. He describes how he did this, with recipes, including a few fermented ones.

Gibbons, Euell, *Stalking the Healthful Herbs*, New York: David McKay Co., 1970.

Discusses many common herbs and their uses. The herbal medicine aspects are discussed, though Gibbons did not trust most of them unless there was a medicinal compound in a particular plant. Tells how to make candies, teas, and an assortment of tasty foods, wines from these herbs.

Gibbons, Euell, *Stalking the Wild Asparagus*, New York: David McKay Co., 1970.

Covers many kinds of wild plants and a few animals, with recipes. A few more wine recipes in this one.

Gouzil, Dezerina, *Mother Nature's Herbs and Teas*, Willits, California: Oliver Press, 1975.

Discusses uses of many plants, often found growing in the west only. Includes recipes for herbs, teas, beers, and a number of wild wines.

Kadans, Joseph M., *Modern Encyclopedia of Herbs*, West Nyack, New York: Parker Publishing, 1970.

This book reads like a centuries-old herbal medicine book, listing all the cures ascribed to every plant. Most plants listed are European, but many are now wild here and others have American relatives. None should be taken seriously as cures, unless verified by modern medical research.

Kingsbury, John M., *Poisonous Plants of the United States and Canada*, Englewood Cliffs, New Jersey: Prentice-Hall, Inc., 1964.

Large listing of plants known or suspected of poisoning man or livestock under any conditions. Many require large amounts or unusual conditions to cause poisoning. Useful for the forager or home winemaker who wants to be creative and try something new. However, if it is not listed in this book that does not guarantee that it is not poisonous.

Lucas, Richard, *Nature's Medicines*, West Nyack, New York: Parker Publishing Co., 1966.

Another herbal medicine book. More concerned with medical drugs found in plants and modern cures with them as well as ancient ones.

Medsger, Oliver Perry, *Edible Wild Plants*, New York: The Macmillan Co., 1945.

A thorough study of edible wild plants in much of the country. Covers Indian, pioneer, and present uses.

Peattie, Donald Culross, *A Natural History of Trees*, Boston: Houghton Mifflin Co., 1950.

Discusses the trees of the eastern United States, including their habitat, growth habits, uses by animals and man. Human uses discussed include lumber and some edible uses.

Scully, Virginia, *A Treasury of American Indian Herbs*, New York: Crown Publishers, 1970.

A listing of Indian plant uses in western North America. The author uses only common names, which are sometimes confusing, but it does give valuable clues to edible and useful plants.

Weiner, Michael, *Earth Medicine*, New York: Macmillan Co., 1972.

Discusses many of the plants in this country that have been used as medicine at some time or other, especially by Indians.

PLANT IDENTIFICATION BOOKS

Bailey, L. H., *Manual of Cultivated Plants*, New York: Macmillan Co., 1949.

This book lists all known cultivated plants of the United States and Canada. It has a few pictures, but is very technical. Its primary use to a home winemaker is to determine what cultivated plants are related to in the wild. For instance, if you have a greengage wine recipe, look greengages up in the index and find that they are related to plums, so substitute wild plums in the recipe.

Courtenay, Booth, and Zimmerman, J. H., *Wildflowers and Weeds*, New York: Van Nostrand Reinhold, 1972.

Attempts to describe plants and flowers in a picture key. Shows many plants of the northeastern United States in beautiful color photos with names and key characteristics.

Fassett, N. C., *Spring Flora of Wisconsin, Fourth Edition*, Madison, Wisconsin: University of Wisconsin Press, 1976.

Includes all flowering plants known as wild plants in Wisconsin and blooming before June 15. This is an example of a localized plant identification manual, which are published in many states. They are useful in that they do not include plants not found in a particular area, so they cut down on identification time and mistakes. They also give more clues on where the plant might be found in the area and when it flowers and has ripe fruit.

Gleason, H. A., and Cronquist, A., *Manual of Vascular Plants of the Northeastern United States and Adjacent Canada*, New York: Van Nostrand Reinhold Co., 1963.

A technical identification manual with no pictures. Lists all known plants of the region, except mosses, algae, and fungi. Not generally useful to an untrained amateur.

Harrington, H. D., and Durrell, L. W., *How to Identify Plants*, Chicago: The Swallow Press, 1957.

Contains a glossary of terms used in plant keys in identification manuals. Also explains keying out procedures and lists a few regional manuals.

Peterson, R. J., and McKenny, Margaret, *A Field Guide to Wildflowers*, Boston: Houghton Mifflin Co., 1968.

This book covers flowers of the northeast and north central regions of the United States. About half the wildflowers are included. This book is built on its pictures, and anyone can take a flower and compare it with the pictures in the book. It is a very useful book for anyone who needs to identify plants. Unfortunately, it doesn't cover every species.

Petrides, George A., *A Field Guide to Trees and Shrubs*, Boston: Houghton Mifflin, 1958.

Discusses all shrubs and trees of northeastern, north central United States and adjacent Canada. Can be used by people with no training, as it includes drawings of twigs and leaves and avoids technical terms as much as possible.

Rosendahl, C. O., *Trees and Shrubs of the Upper Midwest*, Minneapolis: University of Minnesota Press, 1955.

Covers all trees and shrubs, including cultivated, of Minnesota and adjacent areas. Technical, but it includes explanations, some pictures, and a glossary of terms. An example of a localized regional identification manual.

Wilson, C. L., and Loomis, W. E., *Botany, 4th Ed*. New York: Holt, Rinehart & Winston, 1967.

An introductory botany book to give one a better understanding of plant growth habits, types of fruits, flowers, and underground parts.

WINE BOOKS

Appleyard, Alex, *Make Your Own Wine*, London: Maxwell, Love, and Co. Ltd.

Contains a limited number of recipes, almost all from cultivated plants.

Auf der Heide, Ralph, *The Illustrated Wine Making Book*, New York: Doubleday and Co., 1973.

Another useful winemaking book with a lot of information, including preparation of different types of ingredients.

Beadle, Leigh P., *Making Fine Wines and Liqueurs at Home*, New York: Farrar, Straus, and Giroux, 1972.

Gives some history of winemaking, some how-to, and some recipes.

Bravery, H. E., *Home Winemaking Without Failures*, New York: Avenel Books.

Another book originally published in Britain, it contains recipes for many types of wines, also cider, ale, and beer. Does not pay much attention to wild plants, but does discuss growing cultivated fruits for wine.

Delmon, Phillip, *Making Wine Once A Week*, Toronto: Mills and Boon, Ltd., 1973.

Originally published in Britain, this book grew out of a night course taught by the author. (Home winemaking is very big in Britain.) Gives few recipes but discusses process and theory in detail. Also discusses various types (general) of wine in detail.

Gennery-Taylor, Mrs., *Easy to Make Wine*, New York: Gramercy Publishing Co., 1963.

Originally published in Britain, this little volume contains brief directions on winemaking and a number of recipes. It also has tea, syrup, and beer recipes.

Hardwick, Homer, *Winemaking at Home*, New York: Funk and Wagnalls, 1970.

A good book by a longtime home winemaker, gives complete details for an assortment of wine apparatus (including bottle labels). Gives directions for making, blending, bottling and even serving wine. Gives 220 wine recipes, mostly grapes and supermarket fruits.

Kellner, Esther, *Moonshine: Its History and Folklore*, New York: Bobbs-Merrill Co., 1971.

Mostly a history of moonshining in the hills of southern Indiana, including some general history of fermented beverages.

Zanelli, Leo, *Home Winemaking From A to Z*, New York: A. S. Barnes and Co., 1971.

Another British author. This book discusses many winemaking terms and procedures, plus some simplified recipes. A very useful book for the winemaker.

Index

Vitamin C, 46, 93, 95, 120
Vitis vinifera 13

Walnut, 116–118
    black, 116–117
    white, 117
Water-seal. *See* Fermentation lock
Wild rice. *See* Rice, wild

Wintergreen, 112–114, 168–169
Wood violet. *See* Violet, wood

Yarrow, 131–132, 145
Yeast, 15–16, 21, 155

Zanelli, Leo, 131